PRAISE FOR *A MOM LIKE THAT*

Aaisha Alvi's deeply moving, courageous account of postpartum psychosis should be required reading for anyone with a pregnant person in their life. Alvi deftly captures the gravity of this harrowing condition while still rendering the misunderstood, and often misdiagnosed, ailment with tenderness, compassion, and most importantly, hope. I have no doubt *A Mom Like That* will save lives.
— HUDA AL-MARASHI, author of *First Comes Marriage: My Not-So-Typical American Love Story*

A Mom Like That is not only a brave personal narrative, but a bold social commentary. It is well-written and well-informed. Aaisha valiantly — and eloquently — offers her harrowing experience of postpartum psychosis in service of those without a voice to do so. Her struggle to receive appropriate care, despite pleading for it, is a profound example of the racial and cultural biases underlying contemporary disparities in maternal mortality. It is also a product of limited awareness, even among professionals. The delusional thinking underlying Aisha's seemingly intact decision-making can be common in postpartum psychosis, and it is one of the many reasons the disorder can go undiagnosed. Her story provides a jarring example of how such high-functioning individuals can become so ill, and how isolating the experience can be.
— JULIA ALZOUBAIDI, Ph.D., perinatal psychosis program manager, Postpartum Support International

Lessons learned from our own experiences are often the most powerful tool in bringing awareness to others. With great courage and literary skill, Aaisha Alvi does just that. Calling on memories, images, and sensations from her own struggle with postpartum psychosis, she deepens our understanding of this life-altering illness, breaking the shrouds of secrecy, letting the reader in on the realities of psychosis related to childbearing and her lived experience of what it really means to feel insane.

— DIANA LYNN BARNES, Psy.D, PMH-C, editor of
Women's Reproductive Mental Health Across the Lifespan

In her poignant memoir, Aaisha sheds light on the profound challenges of experiencing postpartum psychosis, a condition too often overshadowed by misunderstanding and fear.

Her candid narrative empowers women and families to confront perinatal mental health challenges with compassion and resilience. I hope to use this book to support my patients and their families who are struggling with this condition. This courageous memoir is a beacon of hope for those navigating similar challenges and a vital resource for healthcare professionals striving to deepen their understanding of postpartum psychosis, the most severe and least understood mental health condition a woman can face in her lifetime.

— NICOLE H. CIRINO, MD, reproductive psychiatrist, Texas
Children's Hospital, and professor, Department of Obstetrics
and Gynecology, Baylor College of Medicine

Aaisha Alvi shares a personal and heartbreaking account of her postpartum psychosis, an illness that frequently ends in tragedy. She courageously describes her terror of commanding hallucinations, delusions that seized control of her body and mind, and her struggle against their dominance. The failure to diagnose and appropriately treat the distinct symptoms of postpartum psychosis heralds potential danger for mother and baby. But Aaisha reminds us that postpartum psychosis is a treatable, temporary, and preventable disorder. She tells a story of resilience, a story that simultaneously educates the reader. This book is an inspirational addition to the libraries of professionals who work with childbearing women, lay communities, and growing families.

— MARGARET SPINELLI, MD, clinical professor of psychiatry, Columbia University College of Physicians and Surgeons, and founder and former director, Women's Program in Psychiatry, Columbia University

Aaisha Alvi has written an evocative narrative portraying her lived experiences of postpartum psychosis. The book is rich with insights and details about psychosis and the myriad of ways this mental disorder hijacks thought, perception, emotion; and wreaks havoc in every facet of a birthing person's life.

Alvi educates through this book that's written in easy prose. It is a truth telling. She divulges secret tomes of a temporary "madness." It's clear to see that the protagonist is not at fault, that she is a victim of postpartum psychosis, and the myriad of ways the system can do more harm. This book should be read by psychologists, social workers, physicians, doulas, midwives, OBGYNs as well as those in the social, child services, and law enforcement industries. There simply is not enough education about postpartum psychosis.

— GINA WONG, Ph.D., R.Psych, PMH-C, professor, Faculty of Health Disciplines, Athabasca University, and editor of *Infanticide and Filicide: Foundations in Maternal Mental Health Forensics*

A MOM LIKE THAT

A MOM LIKE THAT

A Memoir of
Postpartum Psychosis

AAISHA ALVI

Foreword by Wendy N. Davis, Ph.D., PMH-C

DUNDURN
PRESS

Publisher: Meghan Macdonald | Acquiring editor: Kathryn Lane | Editor: Megan Beadle
Cover designer: Laura Boyle
Cover image: Unsplash/Navid Sohrabi

Library and Archives Canada Cataloguing in Publication

Title: A mom like that : a memoir of postpartum psychosis / Aaisha Alvi ; foreword by Wendy N. Davis, Ph.D., PMH-C.
Names: Alvi, Aaisha, author.
Identifiers: Canadiana (print) 20240321820 | Canadiana (ebook) 20240321898 | ISBN 9781459754508 (softcover) | ISBN 9781459754515 (PDF) | ISBN 9781459754522 (EPUB)
Subjects: LCSH: Alvi, Aaisha—Mental health. | LCSH: Puerperal psychoses—Patients—Canada—Biography. | LCSH: Mothers—Mental health. | LCSH: Mothers—Canada—Biography. | LCGFT: Autobiographies.
Classification: LCC RG851 .A48 2024 | DDC 618.7/60092—dc23

We acknowledge the support of the Canada Council for the Arts and the Ontario Arts Council for our publishing program. We also acknowledge the financial support of the Government of Ontario, through the Ontario Book Publishing Tax Credit and Ontario Creates, and the Government of Canada.

Care has been taken to trace the ownership of copyright material used in this book. The author and the publisher welcome any information enabling them to rectify any references or credits in subsequent editions.

The publisher is not responsible for websites or their content unless they are owned by the publisher.

Dundurn Press
1382 Queen Street East
Toronto, Ontario, Canada M4L 1C9
dundurn.com, @dundurnpress

This book is dedicated to my mom, dad, husband, and most importantly, my daughter. Without the role each of you played in my life, I never could have survived this illness.

CONTENTS

Foreword xiii

PART 1

1: What's Insane? 3

2: A Little Mad 9

3: I'm Possessed 21

PART 2

4: Breathe 33

5: The Scientific Quest 45

6: Playing the Fool 57

7: The Other Woman 67

8: The Intervention 77

9: The F-Word 87

PART 3

10: Attention Grab 99

11: Loopy Thoughts 107

12: Cinnabon to the Rescue 115

13: Angel of Death 125

14: Kick the Bastard 135

15: Take Two Advils 147

16: Jump 157

17: Hide the Knives 169

18: Sixth Sense 177

19: The Diva You Are 187

20: My Friend Marilyn 197

21: Is This Your Wife? 207

22: Was I Like This? 217

Epilogue 229

Afterword 233

Acknowledgements 245

Notes 247

FOREWORD

IT IS OFTEN SAID THAT SHARING STORIES OF STRUG-
gle and recovery is the very best way to raise awareness and reduce social stigma. Stories have a unique power to create change,
teach, and stimulate compassion. The reality is that when individuals share their truth about mental health symptoms, most
of the time they are met with ignorance, blame, and, at worst,
punishment. The process of breaking through stigma and en-
countering one's prejudice is uncomfortable and unsettling, and
it can feel like a bit of the earth under you has cracked. But what
comes next is new awareness, life-saving change, greater compassion, receptive listening, and the potential to act less restricted
by fear and prejudice. *A Mom Like That* shows what happens
when one individual is courageous enough to share her story,
with the many providers from whom she sought help, with her
family, with the perinatal mental-health community, and now
with any reader of this remarkable story. You've just picked up a
book that will crack the ground of your own misconceptions and
create real change in the most necessary way. Don't put it down;
A Mom Like That will help you become part of the life-saving
change that must happen in our understanding of postpartum
psychosis and recovery.

Each of us, in every family, is susceptible to mental-health challenges and crises, and every community has both risks and protective factors. However, many of us live with the stubborn hope that we personally are not at risk and believe mental-health care is not relevant to us. We often receive implicit messages from family and society that, if such a mental-health crisis does emerge, we must hide it to protect our vulnerability against judgment and scorn. It is a natural human reaction to guard against the fear that mental-health challenges exist for each of us and to protect ourselves using denial and compartmentalization, with an "Us vs. Them" mindset. Most of the time, we don't even realize we're using these mental gymnastics; they're an automatic reaction strengthened by societal messages. However, one experience with a mental-health crisis is enough to make us realize how vulnerable we are. Unfortunately, when a crisis happens, it's also the most difficult time to reach out and find informed help, compassion, and effective treatment to reduce risks and achieve recovery. Aaisha's spell-binding memoir is a genuine illustration of this life-threatening experience and a testament to her own determination and the steadfast support of her family and caring friends.

The risk of postpartum psychosis is not only inherent in its symptoms; the risk is that healthcare providers and families do not know the symptoms, the prevalence, the treatments, and the resources available to treat it, and that risk is compounded by stigma. As Aaisha shares through her story, postpartum psychosis is a uniquely treatable, temporary illness from which women can make a full recovery, with the right care. By sharing her compelling and honest experience, clinical information, and resources for help in this memoir, Aaisha has already improved the level of knowledge and resources available to prevent further crises and ignorance about postpartum psychosis.

The perinatal psychiatric community has made progress in understanding and treating perinatal mental health, including postpartum psychosis. However, no matter how many scientific advancements are developed to improve treatment options and reduce risk, no innovation used by informed providers will help individuals at risk or in a crisis if they and their families are too afraid, ashamed, or escalated to reach out for help and get the treatment they need. In fact, many families initiate contact and make appointments with providers only to cancel or retreat due to a rapid increase in symptoms or, sadly, after a dismissive response. In Aaisha's story, you will see these kinds of experiences and feel the rising panic and risk that such encounters produce. The likelihood of this happening is exacerbated by social stigma and key elements that affect families and providers alike: lack of knowledge and the power of denial and fear. Stigma is tricky — it doesn't always look or feel like judgment; sometimes it feels like we are being reassuring ("You're not that kind of mom."), girding our fear ("Postpartum psychosis is very rare; that would never happen to me. If I see that it is happening to her, I could be vulnerable too."), or guarding against the fear of inadequate professional skills ("I should know how to treat anything in front of me. If I think of this as anxiety, I know what to do.")

For too long, providers have instructed women, families, and colleagues that if an individual feels anxious about their symptoms, they must not be psychotic. Just one page of *A Mom Like That* will show you how wrong that idea is. We have missed the mark in our intention to reassure individuals experiencing perinatal depression, anxiety, or intrusive thoughts by telling them not to worry because "they are not psychotic." While this reassurance might help reduce fear for those living with anxiety, an unintended consequence is that this mistaken either/or dichotomy shames and vilifies the experience of postpartum psychosis at the same time. More dangerously, as Aaisha shows us, it can keep people from receiving the care they desperately need. Mental health professionals can and must provide psychoeducation for families and training for providers that encompasses all of the truth. The best reassurance comes from connection with and care from informed caregivers, including peer supporters and professionals, who each do their part to provide proper psychoeducation, assessment, and treatment. Knowledgeable voices like Aaisha's are bringing that more enlightened communication and intervention to fruition.

Postpartum psychosis is a temporary illness that needs to be understood differently than chronic psychiatric disorders. While the symptoms of postpartum psychosis are severe and present an immediate need for intervention, the disorder is treatable and individuals are capable of full recovery. The news and media, and sadly much of medical education, do not give an accurate representation of the symptoms or outcomes of this disorder, often leaving new parents frightened that they may be "next" with no real pathway to learn more and get the help they need.

As president and CEO of Postpartum Support International (PSI), it is my honour to say that change is happening to better the lives and outcomes for those who may suffer from postpartum psychosis. But there is so much further we need to go. Working together with advocates, researchers, and individuals with lived experience, PSI promotes positive change and justice; increases improved knowledge among attorneys, judges, law enforcement, healthcare providers, and the public about perinatal mental health disorders, including psychosis; and helps change outdated legislation where possible. PSI works to increase public and professional understanding that postpartum psychosis, while it presents a serious and immediate potential for harm, is treatable and temporary.

Aaisha writes eloquently, bravely sharing her transformative story to weave a tale that will change readers' perceptions, just as her ongoing advocacy work has already helped to change entire systems and education for perinatal providers about postpartum psychosis. Her story guides the reader through a raw, first-hand experience that makes accessible an often misunderstood and feared mental health disorder. I believe we are on the cusp of real change in how we understand, treat, and create just social and legal understandings of postpartum psychosis. I believe that cusp of change is here because perinatal mental health providers, researchers, and the medical community are finally starting to listen and learn from survivors like Aaisha and from families who have lost loved ones to this temporary, treatable illness. There is no better information about symptoms, prevention, and urgency than that which we glean from the stories of survivors. Aaisha expresses a truth that many with lived experience have tried to share. We are informed, we will create change through advocacy, but we will do so more quickly and effectively if all of us work together to understand the challenges and prevent the loss, despair, and isolation experienced by far too many women and their families.

Wendy N. Davis, Ph.D., PMH-C
President and CEO of Postpartum Support International

PART 1

1: WHAT'S INSANE?

LINA SAT EYEING ME AS I PUT THE FINAL TOUCHES ON my creation. She gave me an approving smile. Scattered all over my parents' living-room floor were Lego blocks — luckily, they were the larger variety, not the killer small ones. I was feeling more and more like the old me. Today was the first time in over three months that I was actually able to play with Lina. I carefully considered what I should do next, wanting to please her further.

"Mommy, what's insane?" she asked.

My super-duper Lego double-decker on wheels stopped in its tracks. Why was she asking me this? Did she know? And if so, who told her? I felt immobilized by the thought that she knew about me.

"How do you know that word?" I asked, hoping the alarm wasn't evident in my voice.

"I read it in a book that Daddy gave me: *Jane Eyre*." She was scanning, looking for a yellow brick to add to her blue and yellow car.

I wanted to go admonish my husband, Adam. He had taken over feeding Lina's voracious appetite for books while I made my way back to sanity. But to give her a classic for adults was just too much. Though for now, I needed to channel my inner teacher.

"It's when someone gets so sick they lose their mind and can't think properly."

Her Lego car ambled by as she nodded in understanding. "Well if an insane person burns down a house, do you think they are bad?" she asked.

I gulped. I had never read *Jane Eyre* and only knew it was not a children's book. "Is that what happens in the book?"

She nodded.

"Well, it's sad they burn down a house, but they aren't bad, because they are sick." I wondered if this made sense to her five-year-old brain or if I was unnecessarily complicating things.

"That's good, because I don't think an insane person is bad. It's not their fault," she said, smiling and crashing her car into mine.

I didn't know if I should be relieved or intimidated. I opted for intimidated and made a mental note to touch base with Dr. Baker about it, and to talk to Adam about his choice of books for our child.

• • •

As Lina hopped off to engross herself this time in a properly vetted book, I eyed my favourite dish on my mom's kitchen table: I picked out bits of carrot to munch on. Any other time, dipping into the salad bowl with my fingers would have earned me a stern scolding, but not today. I looked up to see my mom's plump round face lined with creases. Her usually neatly plaited salt-and-pepper hair looked frizzy and dramatically loosened, as though she'd been in a brawl.

She looked completely uninterested in the dinner she was prepping, and the kitchen seemed a mess. Dirty pots sat piled in the sink, and vegetable cuttings lay strewn over the table as though someone had thrown them like confetti. Something was up.

"Do you remember Nadia?" my mom asked, toying with the strings of her untied apron.

Dark eyes and smartly manicured nails came to mind. "Wasn't she at the party you dragged me to last week?" I asked.

My mom nodded.

I shook my head; it was just like my mom to worry so unnecessarily about a virtual stranger. *She lives for her kids* was my dad's frequent refrain about her. Ever since the last of my siblings had left home, my mom had begun widening her circle of concern to others, mothering people who seemed to have no one else. I couldn't help but wonder if she was like this because she had been orphaned as a child, forced to quit school before grade eight to care for her younger siblings.

That's probably how she got drawn to Nadia: a new immigrant to Canada, alone with her husband and two kids, one only a newborn.

"I was thinking — you know with you, we never thought — I mean we don't want to make the same mistake — she sounds like you when you were sick," my mom said abruptly.

"What? What do you mean?" I asked. It felt like she'd dropped a bomb and then run away.

"Aaisha, she's miserable. She doesn't want to be anywhere near her kids, keeps going on long walks to get away from everyone and everything. She reminds me of you, when you were sick."

This woman could *not* be like me.

I thought of myself in the midst of my illness, refusing to take a shower unless my mom stood watch in the bathroom so that I wouldn't be trapped alone with the Devil. No, this woman could *not* be like me.

"Tell me everything," I said, a breathless feeling now in my throat.

Her account made me need to pace. Hands clasped in front of me, I walked from the kitchen down the hallway, through the family room and dining room, and back to the kitchen. Their place was best described by the word "cozy." Small and neatly packed with all the essentials a family could ever need, it left you wanting for nothing: shelves filled with books, overstuffed leather seating, a dining table big enough for ten. There was even a "kids' table."

Walking helped me remain calm. I contemplated everything my mom said, trying to stay rational and objective. Hearing that Nadia wanted to run into oncoming traffic made me have to steady myself on the back of one of the dining room chairs. I felt lightheaded.

"Did she say anything about seeing things or hearing voices?" I asked, dreading the answer.

"Well, a couple of times she heard a really angry voice tell her to open the door. But when she did, there was no one there."

I could sense that my mom thought no one being at the door was a good sign; I knew it wasn't. The memory of me only three months earlier overwhelmed me: the urge to plunge a knife into the pregnant belly; the uncontrollable feeling I had to shove smiling, unsuspecting people to their deaths; and then to throw myself into traffic.

From my own experience, I knew what Nadia was experiencing was not only hallucinations but what are known as "command hallucinations." Depending on their content, she could be a risk to herself or others. I remembered the terror I'd had of being commanded by the Devil to butcher my own family.

"We have to get her help!" I yelled, rattling off the symptoms I knew by heart: feeling violent, homicidal, or suicidal. "First it might be 'open the door,' then it might be 'go get the knife,' and then who knows, she might chop off her babies' legs!"

"What's going on?" my dad asked, stepping from the staircase into the hallway. He stared at me as though pure nonsense was coming from my mouth. His brown face darkened as he took in my words.

"Please, we have to get her help. Nadia's really sick. She's gonna kill her kids or something. We need to go over there right now. Please!"

My mom reached for the kitchen phone as my dad, Adam, and I gathered around her.

"Hello. Oh, were you sleeping? Oh, okay; it's just that I was talking to my daughter about you hearing voices, and she thinks that you need to go to the hospital," my mom said. Then she winced. "I'm sorry," she continued. "I was just worried about you. Okay. I'm sorry to have bothered you."

She shook her head at me.

"She's mad at me for telling you about her," my mom said, tension filling her face.

Alarms went off in my head. Nadia was postpartum with a two-month-old, and she was experiencing at least one of the two key symptoms of psychosis: hallucinations. I didn't know if she was experiencing the other one, delusions, but I didn't want to wait to find out. Even having one of the key symptoms was enough to deem an individual psychotic, and I knew that psychosis in the postpartum period was a psychiatric emergency.

Fast shallow breathing was escaping me as I paced, muttering urgently.

"Maybe we can talk to her husband," my dad suggested. "Mikhail's English is not that good, but he knows Pashto," he said, thrusting the phone at Adam, our resident Pashto speaker. My dad knew Pashto too, but he was the opposite of my mom. He was theoretical and abstract, more comfortable with ideas and concepts than with people. While my mom hadn't finished high school, he was an academic.

How two such divergent people came together was via an arranged marriage, typical of that time in India. Nonetheless, their marriage would be the envy of most couples.

Adam took the phone. "Hospital," "very sick," and "danger" were the only words in Pashto I could make out, but his frustrated sighs alerted me to the fact that Adam's attempts to get Nadia help were going nowhere.

"She's gonna kill her babies, she's gonna kill her babies if we don't get over there right away!" It was beginning to look like *I* was the one who needed emergency assistance.

"I'm gonna call the police on her," I said, grabbing my coat as I stomped out of my mom's house, heading for my car. I wasn't sure exactly how I would do that, because I had no clue where she lived. As small as Hamilton was, it was not exactly a hamlet.

From the car, I saw figures hurrying out of my parents' home, still yanking on coats and adjusting their boots. Adam buckled Lina into her car seat, tossing her a new book to read.

"Why don't you go with Mom and Dad to Nadia's, and I'll take Lina home?" he said.

"No, forget that; she can come with us. This is an emergency."

I'd been introduced to Adam twelve years earlier, the summer before I started university. Tall, lanky, and good-looking; three years my senior. I knew from the moment I met him that he was for me.

"Happy-go-lucky from birth" was how his mother described him. And for the most part, that was true. He was the easygoing yin to my perfectionist yang. But growing up under a controlling father had left its mark on him. A decade of marriage had taught me that Adam was unable to deal with conflict or manage plans that veered drastically off course.

I couldn't help but wonder if his offer to take Lina home was that conflict-averse behaviour in action.

2: A LITTLE MAD

THE CHIPPED DOOR OF THE APARTMENT OPENED TO reveal parquet flooring, the type I remembered being popular when I was growing up in the '80s. In the sparse living room, a little boy sat in a tiny blue plastic chair. His face was glued to a TV where a cartoon Dora danced with her monkey friend, Boots. He had one hand in a small metal bowl in his lap. Riveted by Dora, he didn't care that he had visitors. A child-sized mattress lay near him in the corner, upon which I could just make out a small bundle wrapped in a blanket from where I stood in the doorway.

"She doesn't want to come out," Mikhail said, placing his hand on the back of his neck uncomfortably. He had a confused look on his face. I couldn't blame him; there we were: an entourage of five people at his house, close to midnight.

He motioned to the bedroom.

Through the open door I saw a solitary bed pushed against a dingy wall. The narrow window off to the corner was the room's only redeeming feature. Nadia perched stiffly at the edge of the bed, looking like she was working hard to project that she had everything under control.

When I saw Nadia's face, frozen as it was, I wished I hadn't come. I suspected that my mom sensed something too, because she sat down gingerly near her, not even bothering to make eye contact. Pushing past the thought of fleeing, I forced myself to sit closer to Nadia.

She was pretty, prettier than I remembered, even if she did look like an ice sculpture now. Her wide-set eyes balanced rosebud lips and a pointed chin. She was definitely younger than me by a couple of years, still in her twenties.

"I heard you haven't been feeling well," I said, placing my hand gently on her knee. She shifted uneasily.

"You know, after I had my daughter, I felt really bad too. A couple of months ago, after I had a miscarriage, I also felt really miserable and sad."

Hollow black eyes stared straight ahead as though my words had fallen on deaf ears. Recalling from my mom's account that she had heard at least one command hallucination, I took a gamble. "You know, after my miscarriage, I started having these really scary violent thoughts and urges."

"You mean you felt like hurting people?" she asked in a loud whisper, turning to look at me.

Though it was I who had taken the gamble, I was totally unprepared to answer her question. I nodded sheepishly, wondering how she would respond to my confession.

"Me too," she whispered back. More than her words, what struck me was the way she said this, like she was sharing the name of her secret crush — as though relieved to finally be able to tell someone what she had been keeping so close to her heart.

As if on cue to melt the tension, a tiny boy in a cape whizzed past me. It was the boy from the plastic chair. "It's him. I just need to kill Omar and then I'll be fine," she said bluntly, pointing a finger at her son.

I quickly glanced at my mother as her eyes filled with horror and dismay.

"You're having a problem with your hormones, and you need medication to get better. I used to feel like that, but I don't now because I got help. You need medication too," I said, grabbing Nadia's hand.

A deeply pained look replaced the stiffness.

"I don't *want* to kill him, but I *have* to kill him. But I love him. That's why I am going to kill myself instead," she croaked, waving her hand in the direction of Omar, who was still pretending to fly, unaware of what his mother had just said.

My heart felt like it had relocated to my ears as I listened to Nadia confess to any mother's worst nightmare. Though I didn't know what to say, words started falling out of my mouth.

"I felt like that too, Nadia — I felt like killing myself because I didn't want to hurt anyone else. You're not a bad person but you're sick — you need help — medication. It's what made me better."

It felt like she was listening to me, *really* listening to me, but then just as quickly, she wasn't. "What? What is it?" I asked, wondering what I had done wrong.

"It's telling me you're evil and lying. Someone is telling me you are lying. Are you evil, and are you lying?" she asked, turning slowly to look at me with a child-like innocence. The look on her face was an alarming contrast to the murderous confession she had made seconds earlier. The paranoia was taking hold of her.

"What do you think?" I asked, with forced calm.

"I think you're a good person, here to help me," she replied innocently.

"Good, believe that," I said. "Now get ready; we have to go to the hospital."

Getting to my feet, I picked up my winter coat from where I'd just set it down minutes earlier. I breathed a sigh of relief as I pulled on my jacket; this intervention had gone better than I ever imagined.

"I'm tired now. I'll go tomorrow," she said abruptly, stalking off and leaving my mom and me alone in the room with Omar.

I looked at my mother. What had just happened? Everything was going so well, until it wasn't.

Following Nadia, I caught sight of her ushering her husband into the bathroom. A towel over the door blocked it from closing, allowing me to hear her whispering angrily. I wondered what she was saying. I knew all too well the waxing and waning nature of the illness, how she could be insane one minute but seem like she was in full possession of her sanity the next.

From the area between the bathroom and the living room, I was privy to both the heated whispers coming from the bathroom and the antics of the *Berenstain Bears* blasting from the TV. It was a marvel that both Omar, who had followed me out, and Lina could be so engrossed in whatever the bear family was doing, despite all that was going on with Nadia.

The door flew open with an angry bang as Nadia and her husband stepped out. Alarm replaced the confusion I'd seen on Mikhail's face when we arrived. I could tell that Adam had left no detail out in explaining why we were there.

"Come on Nadia, we have to go to the hospital," I said, while Mikhail nodded in fierce agreement.

Nadia turned and stomped off to her bedroom. I followed her.

"See, you've gone and made Mikhail scared of me. Why are you here?" she asked, with a mix of anger and frustration.

"You know why I'm here. You're really sick, and you need to get to a hospital so they can help you."

She was positioned in front of the only window in the room. Recalling my own experience, I couldn't help but wonder whether she was planning to jump. I reached over to put an arm around her shoulder, hoping that would temper the severity of my words. It worked; her anger melted a little as she began to cry softly.

"Come on, I'm here to help you. We're gonna help you get better."

We walked out of her room to the living room, where everyone was uncomfortably assembled. Rapid Pashto flowed from Nadia to Mikhail, his face caught between fear and loyalty.

"Get out of my home!" Her words came through gritted teeth. I imagined that her long nails were drawing blood from the way her hands were fiercely curled into fists.

I saw Lina look up at the sudden outburst.

"Get Lina out of here!" I told Adam. I instinctively felt the need to protect my own flesh and blood from whatever might happen. Following my lead, my parents silently gathered Nadia's children: Omar from his blue chair and the baby from the mattress on the floor. Adam rushed past with Lina in his arms, who looked over at us, alarmed.

Mikhail gawked at the stranger that his wife had suddenly become. As the door slammed shut behind Lina and Adam, Nadia began pacing. With her chest pushed out, she advanced toward me like an animal stalking its prey. Her nostrils flared with every breath she took.

I was beyond frightened. This fraught intervention was working out to be far more than I had bargained for.

"Listen Nadia, you're sick, like I was sick. We just want to take you to the hospital so that you can get better. That's how I got better." I found myself rapidly scanning the area to make sure there wasn't anything for her to pick up and fling at me.

"Please — please just come with us." My voice had lost its confidence. Why had I even bothered to come? I didn't know what I was doing. From my peripheral vision, I caught sight of my parents trying to comfort the kids. Still gawking, Mikhail nodded vigorously.

Though all my energy was focused on Nadia, a sudden burst of maniacal laughter from her made me jump. With her head flung far back and her mouth stretched wide, she cackled with absurd intensity. We all exchanged equally startled glances with each other. There was a wild, monstrous look about her, and I could see how some people might think she was possessed by an evil spirit.

Perhaps this was the break we were all silently praying for. After I nodded my head to Mikhail, we both moved in and gently took hold of Nadia's arms. As though we had planned it, we led her to her shoes and tried to put them on for her. She remained stiffly uncooperative. Frustrated at how she was blocking all my efforts to get her help, I whispered into her ear the first thing that popped into my head.

"Listen, do you want the walls to start talking to you?" I hissed at her. I wanted to kick myself even before the first words fell from my lips. Sure, it was something that I had experienced when I was ill, but it still sounded ridiculous. But by some type of divine grace, her laughter suddenly ceased.

Before my eyes, I saw her undergo a slow shudder that ended with her clutching her heart. "Make them leave," she groaned, before collapsing in a heap at Mikhail's feet.

My mind filled with dread at the thought that Mikhail might force us out of their home.

"Let's go!" said my dad, who recognized that we had reached the end of this clumsy intervention. I knew he was right; we were clearly crossing lines and could get into trouble. But I also knew that I could never live with myself if I left and Nadia ended up killing not only herself, but one or both of her children. It was a risk that I knew was all too real if this illness was left untreated.

I looked around desperately as I struggled to find the right words to say: a sofa, a mattress, some white, stackable plastic chairs, no table. It was evident that they had only recently moved in and had not yet settled into their new home. My eyes caught sight of what had already found its place on Nadia's otherwise bare walls: a plaque with verses in Arabic calligraphy, the type readily available at every Muslim shop.

Propped against Mikhail, Nadia was babbling incoherently. Mikhail looked like he could use something to prop himself up as well.

"Do you love God?" I asked, staring at their choice of artwork. She looked over mid-babble and nodded.

"Your Sustainer has not forsaken you, nor does He scorn you: for, indeed, the life to come will be better for you than this earlier part of your life." I recited the verses by heart in Arabic.

I doubted Nadia knew the meaning of the words I was saying. Most Muslims, including me, committed Quranic verses in Arabic to memory as children without understanding what they truly meant. Still, as I began reciting, Nadia looked up at me and offered me her hand. I took it, telling Mikhail to dial 911.

When Mikhail handed the phone to me, I passed the job of comforting Nadia to him. "She's suicidal, homicidal, and hearing command hallucinations," I said into the phone as calmly as I could manage.

"Stay away from her; we're dispatching the police and paramedics," they advised.

Minutes later, the door opened to Nadia and me holding hands seance-like and calmly chanting in a foreign language.

"So, what's going on here? Is there an emergency?" asked a police officer. He was surveying the sight before him with a mix of curiosity and confusion, as though he'd come to the wrong place. Like a deer caught in the headlights, Mikhail looked over at me. Understanding that he wanted me to be the one to explain the situation, I nodded, and looked at Nadia. She looked at the pack of strangers and then directly into my eyes.

"She's not feeling well. She's hearing voices," I said. "They're telling her to do stuff, stuff she doesn't want to do, and she's feeling homicidal and suicidal."

The image of the seance cracked at once. All eyes locked on Nadia.

"Look at me. Are you hearing voices?" It was the same tall officer speaking. I noticed how big and broad he was, how both officers were like that. Their size was intimidating enough without the guns secured in their holsters. I felt a prickle of uneasiness, never having been in such close proximity to a gun in my life.

Nadia remained sullen and quiet.

"Look at me. Look at me," he said, trying again. Was his voice a little sterner this time? Did it have a hint of anger in it? Or was I imagining it, because I was scared of his gun? As adamant as he was to have her look at him, she was determined not to look at him.

"Come on Nadia, tell them. Look at them and tell them what's been happening to you. They're here to help you. Just look at them," I coaxed gently.

Again, in the same child-like manner as before, she shook her head. I wanted to help her, but I couldn't unless she did some of the work. I knew from experience that what was happening wasn't her fault. I recalled that I'd been terrified of looking at my own doctor when I had been sick, because of the violent urges she triggered inside of me.

"Please just tell them." I was on the brink of tears, overwhelmed by what I had gotten myself into while I was still vulnerable. I had only weaned myself off antipsychotic pills the week before.

Maybe it was the sound of my voice as I pleaded, or maybe she was just frightened enough to believe me, because she slowly looked up. "There's a voice," she began. "He says I have to kill Omar because he will ruin the baby. But I don't want to kill him. I love him. But I have to. But I won't. I'll kill myself instead."

I couldn't have been happier to hear someone confess such terrible things. Even though she was still refusing to look at anyone else, she had been truthful, and I was thrilled.

"And who are you?" the officer asked, turning to me. I knew that was the question in their minds from the moment they first entered the apartment. Nadia seemed to have a strange bond with me, and they wanted to know about it.

"I'm an acquaintance," I said. "I mean, my mother knows her better than I do, because they used to live on the same street. My mom told me that she wasn't well, so I came over to help." I was rambling, and I feared they would suspect that I was as much in need of help as Nadia.

I decided to try again. "I had postpartum psychosis a while back. I heard about her symptoms through my mom and came over because I knew she was in danger." Though I knew it still made little sense, I took comfort in the fact that it was the truth.

It worked. The officers moved aside and two paramedics came forward with the stretcher. It was the first time I noticed that they had brought a stretcher with them. They began fiddling with the straps, the straps I knew they would tie Nadia down with. I didn't want to imagine what this would do to her in her paranoid state.

"Please. Can you please not put her on the stretcher?" I asked. They looked over at me bemused, like I was begging a cook not to use a stove. "She's frightened. I'll hold her hand and we'll walk down together."

I couldn't tell if it was because the lead officer figured I knew what I was talking about or because he just didn't want to lose the gains we'd made, but he nodded in agreement.

"We'll escort them. You guys go ahead, and we'll meet you downstairs," he said to the paramedics. And just like that, they packed up and left.

I hurriedly forced shoes on Nadia's feet while the police took notes. They discussed with Mikhail and my parents what the plan was for taking care of the kids while Nadia was at the hospital.

As we walked to the elevator together, flanked in front and behind by the officers, I kept reciting the verses to Nadia in a whisper. The ride down seemed longer than the one up had been: eight, seven, six, five…. Nadia's grip suddenly tightened, and I caught sight of her darting glances at one of the officer's guns in its holster. It was mere inches away from us.

"I wanna take his gun and shoot him," she whispered urgently, into my face. I wasn't as alarmed as I should have been, because I knew it was a psychotic urge that she didn't agree with.

"It's okay; we are here to keep you safe. We won't let you do that," I assured her in a whisper. I tightened my grip on her hands. The elevator door finally creaked open, as though not wanting to let us out into public.

Red and white lights were bouncing off the front of the building. The spectacle included a police cruiser, an ambulance, and even a fire truck. Mikhail had made his way down on his own and was clutching two car seats, one for the baby and one for Omar. I knew my parents were likely on their way down with the kids.

"One of you needs to come with us," one of the paramedics said, joining us.

"You should go with them," I said, turning to Mikhail.

"No. I want you to come with me," Nadia said. "Please come with me."

I felt uncomfortable, not about going with her, but wondering how Mikhail would feel. He nodded eagerly; problem solved.

"You, sir, can follow us in your car," said the paramedic.

Nadia and I climbed into the ambulance behind him. It was tight inside, worse than the elevator. We squeezed onto benches across from each other, still holding hands. Tubes, oxygen masks, pumps, and tons of other medical supplies I couldn't name hung off the walls. That sterile smell that I associated with hospitals and impending death wafted into my nostrils, making me nauseous.

"Your Sustainer has not forsaken you, nor does He scorn you." We held hands and recited it for what felt like a hundred times. I imagined that the paramedics were itching to tell us to shut up, but instead they ignored us for the most part, murmuring between themselves.

. . .

Nadia was experiencing the most severe postpartum mood disorder: postpartum psychosis. Fortunately, it is not very common; in over a decade of maternal mental-health advocacy work, I have only come across a handful of women who exhibited symptoms of this mental illness each year. However, it is *the* illness that people grappling with a postpartum mood disorder fear the most.

Due to several high-profile cases in the news, this disorder has entered the consciousness of society. There are numerous stories of women with postpartum psychosis who took the lives of their children in unimaginable ways. Names like Andrea Yates,[1] whose five children were drowned; Dena Schlosser,[2] whose baby died after having her arms cut off; and Deanna Laney,[3] whose two sons died after sustaining injuries to the head and whose baby was left severely brain-damaged, are but a handful. All of these women were not only the perpetrators of horrific acts of violence, but also tragic victims themselves; victims of having been misdiagnosed as suffering only from postpartum depression — or worse, undiagnosed altogether.

It is important to add here that postpartum psychosis does not always include themes relating to violence, nor does it always translate into violence. However, the hallucinations and delusions that occur with the illness can take many forms and always loosen one's grip on reality. What makes this illness dangerous in the postpartum period is this loss of reality.

Postpartum depression and postpartum psychosis are on a spectrum of illnesses called postpartum mood disorders. This spectrum of illnesses afflicts approximately one in five women in the year after they give birth. In my work with postpartum moms, time and time again I see their fear of being labelled "a mom like *that*," or of having their children taken away, preventing them from being open about their experiences and concerns during the postpartum period.

This fear is why many struggle for too long with symptoms they should never have to bear alone. It is why, more often than not, the women that I speak with tell *me*, a relative stranger, that I am the first person they have revealed all of their symptoms to. Sadly, this is despite them having loving partners, family doctors who have known them since childhood, or close friends who went through depression or anxiety themselves.

The level of fear women have about this condition is completely unwarranted, and the tragedies that occur need not happen at all. Nothing illustrates this point better than Nadia's story.

3: I'M POSSESSED

BODIES LEAPT OUT OF THE WAY FOR US. EVEN PEOPLE coming to the emergency room recognized that we were in crisis, likely because of the officers and paramedics with us. Still, it looked like everyone in the city had decided on this very day to break a foot, slice a finger, or develop chest pains.

The suffocating, sterile smell washed over me again.

As I tried to help with the triaging process, Nadia kept interrupting with bits of information. "I want to laugh and laugh and laugh," she said urgently, like it was vitally important for the nurse to catch that in her report. She was bringing up completely random, seemingly unrelated topics, like I had done when I was ill. In my experience, it was because I was responding to things going on inside of me.

After we were finally registered, I positioned us in two wheelchairs near the police, who had made themselves comfortable on a bench close to the emergency entrance. Breathlessly, Nadia scanned the people across from us in the waiting area, which I had strategically avoided.

"I want to scratch people with these nails he told me to grow," she said abruptly. I looked down at her nails. Perfectly manicured nails, the ones I had noticed at the party a week ago.

"Who told you to grow them?" I asked.

"The voice, the one that keeps telling me you're evil. He told me to grow them to scratch people." Her command auditory hallucinations were clearly bad, and I knew only too well that she couldn't help but listen to them.

"I feel like grabbing a knife and tearing things apart, and running into the street. Can I show you how I want to run into the street?" she said, jumping to her feet. Her voice sounded pressured, like she would explode if she didn't get it all out quickly.

She was looking and sounding manic, the complete opposite of how I myself had presented both times with postpartum psychosis. I had been quieter than my usual self, some might say zombie-like: talking and moving slowly, deeply introspective about everything I was feeling, sad and anxious. Both presentations make sense, however, because postpartum psychosis often has bipolar disorder underlying it. In a minority of cases, it is a result of severe depression with psychotic features, like mine was.

"I need to show you!" she said again, this time beginning to take off to the waiting area.

"Not now, not right now," I said, forcing her to sit down. I couldn't help but remember my own uncontrollable thoughts and urges — the ones I hadn't *wanted* to do but felt uncontrollably compelled to do. "Listen Nadia, I promise I *won't* let you do those things."

"Promise? Promise? Promise you won't let me?" she asked, the desperation in her voice palpable.

"I promise."

Her body slumped as though a huge weight had been lifted off her. But the relief was short-lived. "Promise me you won't let me do those things, okay? Promise me, okay?" she begged again.

"I won't let you run into the street; I won't let you take a knife and run around; I won't let you scratch people," I repeated, in an attempt to comfort her.

22

"But how? How are you going to do that?" she asked. "You are too small. You are way too small to stop me. I'm so much bigger than you. How are you going to stop me?" Her voice was rapidly escalating, getting louder and louder.

I motioned with my head to the police. "I'll get them to stop you," I said, hoping to end the discussion.

She scoffed. Then "No, *you* have to stop me!" she screamed. Despite their size and their guns, in her mind there was still more of a chance that I could control her than that they could. "Take a rope and tie me up. That's how you can stop me. Let's get a rope," she suggested.

"I'm not going to do that," I said.

She was exhausting. I was exhausted. I thought about how I'd been told to get proper sleep and not get overtired, especially since I was still recovering from exactly what Nadia was suffering from. I couldn't figure out why it was taking so long for her to be seen by a doctor.

"You have to," she declared furiously. "I'm possessed. Can't you see that I am possessed? I have really strong powers."

I knew right away she was experiencing the most frightening symptom that I'd endured, when a psychotic individual feels like their thoughts, urges, and sometimes actions, are coming from someone other than themself.

Finally, when we had been sent to a private examination room, Mikhail and Adam arrived. I wondered if they had put us in this room on purpose, instead of putting us in the large ones where patients were simply screened off with curtains, affording little privacy. Whatever the reason, I felt grateful for the room, which had a leather sofa and armchair, and was cozier and less sterile than the others.

"She's been placed under arrest for expressing homicidal thoughts," Adam said, when he was able to get me out of the room.

Recognizing the dread in my face, he took my hands between his and continued. "They'll drop the charges once the doctor confirms she's sick and they admit her for treatment. You did good today, honey, really good," he said, pulling me into a hug.

A piece of my own illness that had never made sense suddenly fell into place. I realized now why my doctor had refused to "lock me up" when I had been begging for it. The doctor had bristled at my request, saying that she would need to involve the police without a psychiatrist on hand to facilitate my admission to the mental-health unit of a hospital. At the time, what she was saying hadn't made any sense to me. I knew now that she was saying the police could have brought me in and done to me what we were doing to Nadia. At that point I would have welcomed police intervention, because of how bad things were, but I couldn't help but feel guilty about the present turn of events.

We went back into the room. Mikhail and Nadia were huddled together on the sofa, and he was gently rubbing her back. Avoiding looking at Mikhail, I wondered if he would hate me for the rest of my life for having involved the police in this way. Nadia turned to me, relieved to have me back. Positioning myself in the armchair across from her, I sat holding her hands. Innocence flooded back into her face, but there was something else there too, something I couldn't quite put my finger on.

"What's wrong?" I asked.

She hesitated. After all that she'd told me, I couldn't understand what could be left, what was so awful that she didn't want to share.

"Am I a good person?" she finally asked. My cheeks felt hot, like I had just been slapped across my face — hard. Of all that had transpired that evening, nothing shocked me more than this question.

I felt myself flash back to three months earlier.

· · ·

24

"Am I a good person?" I had asked Adam. "Am I a good person?"
I asked everyone I saw that entire day. It was the first day that I'd
been sent home with medications for whatever was plaguing me.

I wanted an answer, a real answer to what felt like the most pressing question of my life. I wanted someone to tell me that what I was
experiencing, the homicidal and suicidal thoughts and urges, had
nothing to do with me as a person and was attributable to something
else, someone else, *anything* else. But at the time, all I could elicit was
gentle, unwittingly condescending pats on the head, nothing that
told me that what was happening wasn't my fault.

"Of course you're a good person," whomever I asked would
respond.

"But sometimes you're mean, like when you took the last samosa," my brother would say on occasion, flashing me a teasing smile.

• • •

I thought of that painful day. "Listen, Nadia. You're a wonderful
person. Look at the beautiful healthy kids you've raised. Look at
your husband who loves you. Of course you're a good person! You're
a good person, but right now you are sick. That's why you feel the
way you do."

It was a bittersweet moment. It felt good to be able to help someone hear the words I had so desperately wanted to hear, but at the
same time, my satisfaction was mixed with the sadness of knowing
I hadn't heard those words myself when I needed them.

"So, what brings you all here today?" the young man asked,
bursting in. He wore blue scrubs and held a clipboard, but it was
the stethoscope draped over his neck that tipped us off that he was
a doctor, likely a resident, given the hour.

Nadia immediately straightened up, this time ready to answer.
I was pleased that I had peppered all our talks, beginning with the

ambulance ride over, with reminders to tell the doctor *everything* that was on her mind if she wanted to get better fast. I suddenly realized that she had really taken this advice to heart, because she had been giving me insight into every single hallucination and delusion plaguing her.

We waited with bated breath. "It's all because of her," she said, an accusatory finger pointing at me. "She's the reason I'm sick. Somehow she seems to know what's going on in my head, and it's because she came to my house that I got sick. That's why I'm here."

Her thoughts were clearly disorganized, something I had also dealt with. I had believed that my family was going to act on the violent intrusive thoughts in *my* mind when I was ill. This type of bizarre thinking was yet another symptom of postpartum psychosis. I hoped this doctor, even though he was just a resident, could see that.

Nevertheless, "mortified" would have been an understatement to describe how I felt.

"No, no, that's not it," I countered.

The doctor's eyes focused on me, and suddenly I feared being committed to a hospital myself.

"Look, she's right that I had an idea about what was going on in her head, and that was why I showed up at her house. But the only reason I knew that was because I had postpartum psychosis myself a couple of months back." I tried to sound calm, though I was feeling anything but. "I'm recovered now, but I did have it, and that's how I knew she needed medical help. She has a lot of the same symptoms I had."

"What type of medication were you on?" he asked, scribbling something on his clipboard.

"Effexor, Klonopin, and Seroquel. But I'm off Klonopin and Seroquel. Now I just take Effexor." I held my breath.

His attention drifted back to Nadia.

"Do you know what year we're in?" he asked.

"It's 2006," she said.

"What month is it?

"December."

He nodded. I was impressed by the clarity of her answers. I knew these were routine questions to see how with it she was. I couldn't remember how I'd answered them when I was ill.

"So, what type of symptoms are you having?"

Nadia supplied most of the answers, Mikhail contributed a few, and I reminded her of some of the things she had told me.

"Do you have any allergies?" he asked.

She shook her head.

"I'm going to give you an injection to calm you down and some antipsychotic medication to take tonight. You're going to have to stay here for a bit."

I nodded my head and Nadia nodded in agreement. A shot of Ativan and an antipsychotic pill later, she was fast asleep.

Adam and I left the hospital at three o'clock and were back again by eight the same morning. Nadia had been admitted to the mental-health ward. I knocked on her door before entering. Nadia managed a weak smile when she saw me. Noting that Mikhail wasn't there, Adam volunteered to let us have some time alone together.

Her room was big, and the bed next to hers was empty; thank goodness for that. There was little else there except for the bed on which she was lying. I had spent a lot of time in and out of hospitals because my in-laws suffered from kidney disease and cancer, and I noticed that her room was unlike theirs. No strange tubes or equipment were hooked up to the walls, and even her bed looked bare, almost spartan. I guess the barrenness was intended to keep the patients who needed to be in such rooms safe from themselves.

I had also noticed one other big difference on this trip to the hospital: the double doors Adam and I had come through to get to this side of the building bore a large sign saying that they were alarmed. I had never seen such a sign when I visited my in-laws, no matter which wing they were in.

"The voice is still there, but he's not as loud as he used to be," Nadia confided. "Also, I don't think I need to be tied down anymore," she added shyly.

I smiled, and sat holding her hand as she dozed in and out of sleep. "You're evil, I hate you," she'd say occasionally when she woke. "I — I don't mean that," she'd say just as quickly. "It's *him*," she'd say, pointing at her head. "He's forcing me to say that. He really hates you."

"It's okay," I said, giving her hand a squeeze. By the time Mikhail came, she was fully awake. I offered to step out of the room, but didn't, at Nadia's insistence. They spoke in Pashto. I didn't even try to make out what they were saying, instead pretending to be deeply preoccupied with a large dark spot on the floor.

I contemplated all the awful details he was likely filling her in on: that I had gotten her arrested, even though the charges had been dropped; that she would be in there for days, if not weeks; that they had nobody to watch their kids for that long. The sound of a throat being cleared brought me out of my negative thoughts. Mikhail and I had exchanged roles: he was now in charge, and I was playing the part of the stricken deer in headlights.

"You know, I don't know what to say to you," he said, in halting English.

I noticed his thick accent for the first time, and his voice sounded harsh. I cringed and glued my eyes back onto that mesmerizing black spot on the floor, waiting for the rest of it.

"If your mom didn't tell you something was wrong — and you didn't bring Nadia to the hospital. I don't know what would have happened."

I looked up at him and saw that his eyes were soft and bright.

• • •

Postpartum psychosis is undoubtedly a frightening illness to have, but it does not necessarily need to be feared. Unfortunately, in my opinion, the stance taken by some organizations focused on maternal mental health fuels unwarranted fear. In their attempt to protect and shelter new moms, they opt to minimize the existence of this condition out of fear that it may unnecessarily frighten women. Due to this, many organizations have the tendency to refer to it as a "rare"[1] event, or worse, "very rare."[2]

Though it is *relatively* rare when compared to other postpartum disorders, its incidence is actually on par with the incidence of having a child with Down syndrome or cerebral palsy. Postpartum psychosis[3] occurs in one to two out of every one thousand deliveries, Down syndrome[4] occurs in one in seven hundred live births, and cerebral palsy[5] occurs in two to three out of one thousand live births. Given that postpartum psychosis can also occur after pregnancy loss or miscarriage, its incidence is not that unusual.

Nobody would suggest that people need not know about Down syndrome because it is "relatively rare." In fact, most women who give birth after thirty are told of its very real possibility and given the option to be tested for it. Why? Because knowledge is power, and it enables women to be better prepared in the event such a circumstance finds its way into their lives.

Although there is a real concern that hearing about an illness like postpartum psychosis can escalate anxiety or suicidality in already depressed or anxious women, I firmly believe the remedy for this is more information, not less. When met with ignorance and misinformation, misdiagnosis and dismissal can result in not only suicide, but also infanticide and other unspeakable tragedies.

The reality is that nobody can be frightened into developing postpartum psychosis, just as no one can be frightened into having a child with cerebral palsy or Down syndrome. In over a decade of supporting women with postpartum mood disorders, I have yet to see a mom whom I educated about the symptoms of postpartum psychosis go on to develop it just because she was informed of the condition. Moreover, developing the condition is not a death sentence. This is also an important fact I share with families — that even in a worst-case scenario, when a woman does have postpartum psychosis, the condition is temporary and entirely treatable.

It is the tragedies that result from ignorance about this condition that really make it something to fear. This is why it is so important for the average person to know about this condition the same way they know about Down syndrome or cerebral palsy. This way, people can speak openly about what they are experiencing or witnessing in a loved one, without the fear of being misunderstood. Only when society is better informed about the reality of this illness can people seek help for its symptoms and advocate for proper care in the face of ignorant or indifferent healthcare professionals.

PART 2

4: BREATHE

FIVE YEARS EARLIER

I paced my living room, the slate tiles that I'd fallen in love with when I first saw my condo cold under my feet. The cloudy blue walls nicely complemented the floors, or so I thought. I wasn't that good at interior design but hoped one day my home would look the way I imagined it.

For now, my living room held a few of my furniture choices. A brown leather sofa that was nice and streamlined — I hated those fat pneumatic ones — a chaise, and a mustard-coloured papasan wicker chair that was Adam's parents', a relic from the '70s. There was also a Japanese-style coffee table and several shelves filled with books. It wasn't possible to be my dad's daughter and not have a personal library.

Why was Adam taking so long? I didn't know how he'd managed to convince me to let him look at it first. The bathroom door burst open, and Adam came out grinning like the Cheshire cat.

"My boys can swim!"

We melted into hugs. We had overcome my former doctor's concern that I'd need fertility drugs to get pregnant. She suspected that my naturally high prolactin levels would make my body think I was already pregnant or lactating.

PART 2

I was ecstatic. I had always dreamed of having my own kids. Nine months went by in a blur. Whereas many of my friends hated their pregnant bodies, I found my stretching stomach to be beautiful. It was wondrous to see more than ribs when I gazed at my unclothed body in the mirror.

Two weeks before my due date, while *Harry Potter and the Philosopher's Stone* sat perched on my mountainous belly, I saw it undulate. I slid the book off to see my belly contract violently like the Loch Ness monster was moving beneath my skin. Weird, I laughed.

That evening the undulating continued, and it felt like my stomach was tightening and releasing at different intervals. There was no pain, just rhythmic contractions getting closer and closer together. Was I in labour?

I recalled the screaming and weeping I had witnessed when I went in with my sister, Mariya, as she delivered my niece. I couldn't possibly be in labour. Labour was pure hell.

Either way, it seemed like a good time to scrub the nursery. A pine crib that could convert into a toddler bed, and then later even into a double bed, welcomed me. Crisp, white eyelet bedding adorned it. The dresser had a top that folded down into a diaper-change table, and it displayed a full array of stuffed animals, including Winnie the Pooh, a pair of hippos, birds, a seal, bears, and a tiger. It was a veritable menagerie of stuffies.

I busied myself wiping this and that, then moved over to Lina's bookshelf, already filled with board books. Picturing myself reading to my little one, I picked up the monkey sitting on a pile of books he appeared to be hoarding for himself. "Ooo, ooo, ooo," he grunted as my thumbs squeezed his belly. Adam had bought it for Lina, his soon-to-be baby monkey.

The pulsing continued through the remainder of the night. "I think I'm in labour," I confided excitedly to Adam. We were sitting on our bed together.

"I thought you said labour was crazy painful and you'd be screaming like a banshee." He looked perplexed. I had described the horror of Mariya's delivery with animated renditions of the screams so many times that he couldn't believe labour could be so quiet.

"Watch," I said, getting to my feet and pulling from my pocket the clunky purple stopwatch that I'd been using to time myself. Lifting my top so he could see my bare belly, I could tell that he could feel it tightening under his hands, because he looked over at me, surprised. I nodded.

"Every four minutes for sixty seconds," I said.

"I think I'm in labour," I said into the phone a few minutes later. I had called the labour and delivery number and was giving the nurse all the details.

"Wait, this is your first baby, you're not having any pain, and you think you're in *labour*?" I could hear the receiver being covered and muffled laughter as my words were shared with others.

"Wait 'til you have *pain* that's every four minutes for sixty seconds." She hung up.

I lay in bed, embarrassed.

"It's okay, honey, soon," Adam said. He didn't know how true his words would be.

Pop. What was that? I got up and a small gush of liquid spilled out of me.

• • •

"My name's Aaisha and my water just broke. I'm the one who called a few hours earlier and you said wasn't in labour," I explained at the labour and delivery triage desk. It was four in the morning, and I knew it was either this woman, or the one that sat next to her, who had laughed at me. The young nurse didn't seem in a laughing mood as she ushered me quickly to a bed and asked me to remove my clothing from the waist down so a doctor could examine me. She drew curtains around me.

"You are in full active labour, seven centimetres," the doctor said, emerging from between my legs.

I could tell. The pain had just kicked in and I was screaming like Mariya had.

"I need the epidural," I shrieked into Adam's face, pulling him by the front collar of his shirt.

"But we don't need that," he said, reminding me of my birth plan, the one that said we could do it without an epidural. What did he mean, *we*? It was me who was in bloody agony.

"Breathe, like we learned in Lamaze," he said, smiling encouragingly.

Right, breathe. I needed to breathe through the pain. But blankness filled my mind.

"How do I breathe?" I said. Blankness stared back at me.

"I need the epidural," I shrieked again. I was dying.

I was moved to a delivery suite, an unusually big room with its own bathroom. It was the same one I had watched my sister suffer and give birth in. I wasn't suffering now; I had just gotten the epidural and was in bliss, sipping water and crunching ice. Why had I ever debated the pros and cons of this miracle drug — God's gift to womankind?

The room was sparsely furnished with a big birthing bed with guardrails like jail bars. I guessed the bars were there in case us moms-to-be wanted to escape from the inevitable pain. It would have been neat to have the ceiling of the room covered in adorable baby pictures as reminders of what awaited us. I couldn't wait to meet my baby.

· · ·

Five hours later in my recovery room, I was looking down at Lina. She wasn't looking at me, though. She was sniffing my breast searching for something to quench her thirst.

"I want another one," I said, gazing lovingly at Lina.

"Let's hold off on that thought for a bit," Adam said, coming to join me.

Thirteen stitches felt worth it. Where they could put thirteen stitches down there was beyond me, but I wasn't about to go looking to find out.

"You need to pee," the nurse said, coming to help me from my bed. Adam had stepped out to get me the jumbo pads I'd "forgotten" to buy. Except I hadn't actually forgotten to buy them. When I saw how diaper-like they were, I'd convinced myself the regular ones would do. Not so, apparently.

I wobbled to the washroom, supported by the nurse. Though they were really nice about it, I couldn't get my head around the fact that nurses kept coming in to pull away my top and examine my nipples, even tweak them, or remove my blanket to comment on how badly swollen my parts were.

"Gosh, I think you're the tiniest person I've seen give birth to a normal-size baby without having a C-section," one nurse commented.

I felt like a circus spectacle. How come nobody ever mentions that your right to dignity vanishes the moment you give birth?

The nurse stood in the doorway waiting for me to pee. Meanwhile, I was tired, sleepy, and then suddenly in a dark tunnel. It was exactly like the *Reader's Digest* descriptions of near-death experiences, except there was no light beckoning me forward.

"She passed out!"

I heard gasps and clatters. I opened my eyes to feel myself being lifted onto the hospital bed. I needed to tell them what had happened. I had not passed out, I had *died*. I recalled the dark lonely tunnel and travelling somewhere before they brought me back.

"I died," I said suddenly. Five pairs of eyes looked over at me mid-bustle to safely put me in bed.

"I died," I said again.

"No. You passed out because you lost two pints of blood giving birth," said the nosy nurse who had wanted to hear me pee.

I felt confused. What was up with the tunnel, then? I'd fainted before when I had iron problems, but I never went into a tunnel at that time.

An IV bag of Pitocin came to make my acquaintance, to stem the bleeding by forcing my uterus to contract rapidly. That effectively ruined the rest of my day as harsh contractions overwhelmed me. It was the torture of labour all over again, but this time I had nothing to look forward to after the pain.

"I want an epidural," I recalled screaming to no one in particular. It didn't matter; I never got one.

Later, a nurse with a tag that said "Diana" came in. She was Jamaican and had a friendly face and wide smile. "Hey, hon. We're gonna put a catheter in you so you don't have to get up to pee," she said.

I looked up at her, unable to stem the flow of tears. I hated medical interventions, probably because I'd been poked and prodded my whole childhood while doctors tried to figure out why I was so small. To the doctors of that time, I was an enigma. My limbs and all other parts of my body were perfectly proportional to my small frame, but I just didn't seem to grow much. One doctor even suggested I take growth hormones to grow bigger. The seventies were weird like that.

"I don't want a catheter," I said tearfully. "I'm scared of it."

"Aw, honey," she said. "We just don't want you to get hurt falling down, that's all."

I nodded. "I wish I could just pee in bed and not have to get up," I said sadly.

Diana was quiet, watching the mess of a human being I was, bawling like a baby.

"Look," she said finally. "I'm gonna put some pads under you, and I want you to just pee in bed like you said. I will clean you all up. I'm gonna make it so you don't need a catheter," she said.

I looked up at this woman, a true angel. I wanted to give her a hug.

I peed in the bed, and true to her word, she cleaned me up.

After three days in the hospital to make sure all was well and that I knew how to get the baby to latch and feed like an expert, I left, looking like a ghost more than a new mom. My skin finally matched the colour of those Fair & Lovely skin bleaching commercials I used to laugh at. It was a look Indian society craved. Who knew all it took was losing copious quantities of blood?

· · ·

"She's such a good feeder, and you have such a good latch," Mariya said, smiling and coming over to take a peek at her niece, my newborn baby girl. It was true, she'd drink for forty minutes on one side and then drink some more from my other breast.

"I feel like a cow. Call me milk mama," I said chuckling. "Moo."

I sat on my mom's living room sofa, taking it all in. Though I found it hard to believe Lina was actually mine, we had an undeniable bond. I instinctively knew when she would start fussing and need to be fed just by how my breasts would feel. Sometimes they'd even leak.

Things were objectively going well, really well, for me. Lina was a good feeder, I had a healthy milk supply, and she was peeing and pooping on schedule. Nevertheless, things just didn't feel right. I kept having the same gnawing thought stuck in my head.

"How do I know if she's drinking enough?" I'd say randomly at least four times a day.

"Because she's peeing and pooping," my mom would say with a laugh, shaking her head like I was just being silly.

"But how do I know she's getting enough milk from me?" I'd ask.

"Because she's peeing and pooping," Adam would repeat. He'd look at me quizzically, single eyebrow raised.

"I wish there were some kind of gauge on the side of my boob," I announced, gazing at Lina, who was suckling away contentedly. "Then I'd know for sure."

"I can't believe this is like her tenth pee diaper," Adam announced one evening. "This kid is like a hose," he laughed.

Adam was sweet. Lina was two weeks old, and I hadn't changed a single diaper. He'd fully embraced papa-hood and actually seemed delighted to do his part, even if that part was changing a gazillion diapers. I was relieved. I hated the coiled dried umbilical cord that newborns have. I couldn't bear the thought of seeing or tending to it for those first weeks until it fell off.

The nagging worry that she might not be getting enough to drink pervaded my mind from the moment I woke up until I went to sleep. I began to chronicle her feeding sessions religiously in a cute little pink notebook my best friend, Zara, had given me.

Time: 3:43 p.m.	Side: Right Breast	Length: 35 minutes
Time: 5:15 p.m.	Side: Left Breast	Length: 40 minutes
Time: 6:05 p.m.	Side: Right Breast	Length: 15 minutes

I'd scan it periodically several times a day, just to make sure I wasn't starving Lina.

"What's wrong? Why are you crying?" Adam asked one day.

I was sitting across from him, watching him cuddle Lina and whisper sweet nothings to her.

"Nothing," I said, getting even more choked up.

It was true. I didn't know why I was crying. I was confused. I wasn't exactly sure why I was sad; I was just sad. Was it because I didn't know if Lina was getting enough to drink? I didn't know. Was it because Adam seemed to have it all figured out? I didn't know. Was it because I was feeling jealous of Adam's relationship with Lina? I didn't know. All I knew was that I was sad and it was getting worse.

My mom had demanded I follow Indian cultural protocol and stay at her house for forty days after having Lina.

"What's the problem? Mariya stayed, why can't you?" she'd announced, months before I delivered. Her hands were on her hips, ready for a fight. Her apron dangled in front of her like a shield. The fight wasn't going to be with me though; it was going to have to be with Adam.

"Forty days? Who does that?" he'd said, smacking his forehead for added effect. "Jeez, we're not in some village in India!"

My mom won out in the end, and our home for the month was my parents' crowded gloomy basement. It was an eclectic mishmash of cast-away items from the rest of the house. My mom's childhood as an orphan was, I hypothesized, what didn't permit her to get rid of things she no longer needed. Instead, in an extremely organized manner, she held on to everything lest it ever be needed by someone else at some other time.

I remember one Christmas when my sister and I were invited to a fairytale-themed costume party. We'd agreed to go dressed as fictional characters from the same story. The only problem was that we'd procrastinated until Christmas morning, and all the stores were closed. Being super-competitive, I wanted to win — badly.

"Now we have nowhere to go to get things for our costumes!" I had exclaimed, annoyed.

"Why don't you look in the basement; there's lots of things down there," my mom offered.

"It's for a costume party! We need weird things, like freaky wigs and bear paws and stuff," I said, rolling my eyes in exasperation.

"Well, we can check it out at least," suggested Mariya. She was far more creative and willing to take a risk when it came to things like that.

We went to the party later that evening dressed as the grandma and the wolf from *Little Red Riding Hood*. Even though some people had purchased fancy costumes, we won for having the most creative costumes, courtesy of my mom's haute-couture basement collection.

. . .

My mother expecting me to stay with her after I had my baby was not as outlandish as it might sound to some. This expectation is traditional in many societies and cultures worldwide.[1] All over India, going to stay at the maternal home for anywhere up to three months postpartum is common. During this time, new mothers are treated to rest, warm baths, oil massages, and foods cooked to heal the body and help stimulate milk production. Similar practices can be found all over the world, including East Asia, Africa, Latin America, and among Indigenous communities.[2]

Though the individual practices differ across cultures, almost all of these traditions include a period of mandatory rest, nourishing foods, and ample care and support from loved ones.[3] These practices were never meant to ward off or mitigate postpartum mood disorders, but they provided time for the mother to be mothered herself and get rest and support. On their own, these are all noble goals that every new mother I have supported would readily welcome.

• • •

Mariya settled down beside me one evening a few days later. I was curled up on the basement couch alone while Lina was sleeping in the other room — our bedroom for the month. Mariya was older than me, but not by much. We'd shared bedrooms for the bulk of our childhood and knew each other really well. There are no real secrets when you don't have a wall separating you from your sibling.

Not having an actual physical wall didn't stop us from laying down an imaginary one in our room, especially in our teenage years. But aside from a few years when we drifted apart, we were as close as sisters could be. I idolized her, even though I would never have admitted it to her face.

Even Adam recognized how much I looked up to her. "I can't believe you chose the exact same furniture as your sister when we got married," Adam would regularly say before climbing into bed. I would always turn red and feel stupid, but it kind of summed up what my relationship to her was: I was a copycat.

• • •

"How come you're sad? Tell me," Mariya coaxed.

I shrugged. I didn't know, but just by virtue of her asking, the tears I'd been keeping dammed up started a slow march down my face.

She straightened herself up and put her arm around me. "Are you feeling a little neglected by Adam?" I hadn't ever thought of that before. "It happens sometimes."

Maybe she was right. Maybe I felt neglected because I was jealous of Lina. Maybe that's why I was sad. I wasn't sure, but it was possible. I grabbed a cushion from beside me to cover my face. I didn't want her to see me full-out crying. I refused to move the pillow and talk.

"Look, I'm headed back to Buffalo," she said. "Call me if you wanna talk, okay?" She gave me a kiss on top of my head. "Love you," she said, before leaving.

I just kept on crying. Even though I wasn't convinced that I was sad because I was jealous of my daughter, I hated myself.

The sadness continued and worsened — worsened, because I now suspected that maybe I was subconsciously jealous of Lina. Although I didn't really feel jealous, I sometimes cried when I saw Adam with Lina. I figured that could be the reason. After all, I was into my third week postpartum, past the "baby blues" period, which usually only lasted two days to two weeks. You couldn't just feel sad without there being any reason, could you?

• • •

It is often difficult for women to make sense of why they are feeling the way they do even after the normal "baby blues" period of adjustment. It's a common question I am asked in my work, especially by women who have never before struggled with their mental health. Though no one knows for sure why these mood changes occur, there are more and more studies seeking to find answers.

For now, some suggest it has to do with the crash in pregnancy hormones that happens after giving birth.[4] Others believe it may have to do with actual physical changes the brain experiences in pregnancy, with gray matter shrinking.[5] And yet other brain-imaging research hypothesizes that the anxious neural responses parents normally have to their babies' cries, which help us anticipate and prepare for danger, are heightened beyond the normal range in some women.[6] This can trigger disturbing thoughts, distressing anxiety, and depression. Hopefully, more research in the area will offer greater insights.

5: THE SCIENTIFIC QUEST

"TA-DA!" ADAM ANNOUNCED ONE EVENING. HE placed a big bowl of popcorn in my lap as I sat in the basement contemplating the extent of my sadness.

"So, what will we be watching tonight?" Adam asked, holding up three DVDs: *Planes, Trains and Automobiles* was one of them — my all-time favourite.

"You pick," I said listlessly, shrugging.

Planes, Trains and Automobiles it was. He popped it in. Lina suckled away contentedly at my right breast, her preferred side. She looked so serene, her cheeks and mouth bobbing in and out guppy-like, making a clicking sound. I could even hear tiny gulps on occasion.

> *Soft pulsating fontanel. Long iron handrail. The soft top of her fragile skull colliding with the edge, the unusually pointy edge of the handrail along our basement stairs. Blood pouring out of the jagged puncture wound.*

I gasped. Lina let out an ear-piercing shriek and unlatched herself. She looked up at me, wild-eyed. Clutching her tightly against my body, I ran up the basement stairs, shuddering as I passed the handrail.

"Here, Mom, I think she wants you," I said breathlessly, before racing down again. Why did I just see an image of Lina's head being smashed in by a handrail, and who was it that did the smashing? Was it me? I hadn't seen myself doing it, but who else could it have been?

Adam was just sitting there, mouth hanging open — dumbstruck by what he'd witnessed. The movie wasn't even paused.

"What just happened here?" he finally asked, confusion written all over his face.

"Nothing," I lied, trying my best to look calm. I knew it likely wouldn't work, because I was never the best at hiding my emotions. It didn't help that I was gifted with Lily Collins–style eyebrows, but this was long before Lily was popular or thick eyebrows were coveted. Though thick eyebrows were often touted as making you look youthful and innocent, they made me appear perpetually worried.

Adam looked at me, his own eyebrows raised. He knew I was lying.

"Can you come to the bedroom?" I asked, taking his hand and leading him next door. It too was an eclectic mix of cast-off furniture, but at least it was less cluttered. I motioned for him to sit on the bed and positioned myself on his lap. Stroking his cheek to endear myself to him before the big confession, I started to speak. I wasn't quite sure of what I would say — that I had seen that horrific image, that I was scared that somewhere inside me I wanted to hurt Lina.

Instead, I heard myself say: "Remember how things used to be before we had Lina? Remember how much fun we used to have?" My lips quivered a bit as I recalled the image again.

Soft pulsating fontanel. Long iron handrail. The soft top of her fragile skull colliding with the edge, the unusually pointy edge of the handrail along our basement stairs. Blood pouring out of the jagged puncture wound.

Was it me? Was what I saw something that I wanted to do? Could I really do something like that to my own flesh and blood? Would I end up doing something like that to my innocent baby?

"Remember? Life was fun, right?" I persisted, in spite of the questions swirling in my mind.

"What are you talking about? What are you trying to say?" Adam said, making a move to get up.

I slipped off his lap. There was a sudden harshness in his voice that I wasn't used to.

"What on earth are you trying to say?" he demanded again, his voice rising. He was standing now, and was he shaking a little? I couldn't be sure.

"It's just that, I think maybe Lina should be with someone else. Maybe it's not good for us to keep her. There are so many people in the world that can't have kids. Why not give her to one of *those* moms?" I said. I had come up with the only viable solution to the problem growing in my mind, the problem of me being a potential threat to our baby.

"Are you crazy or something?" he yelled, his face reddening. There was no doubt about it, he *was* shaking and, as his six-foot frame towered over me, I suddenly noticed how tall he was. I had never seen him like this in all my years of being married to him. "You definitely need to stop nursing. It's obviously making you crazy," he muttered, sweeping past me out of the bedroom.

"What's happening?" my mom said, carrying the baby in. Lina had started crying, and I recognized the alarm in my mom's eyes

47

at seeing my tear-stained face. Adam came back and took Lina to comfort her.

"I'm gonna go out to get Aaisha a breast pump. Mom, can you stay down here with them while I'm out?" Though he was talking to my mom, Adam's voice still had an angry edge to it that I could tell he was trying to soften.

"Why? She nurses Lina," my mom said perplexedly, looking from me to Adam.

"Not anymore," he said, "It's too stressful. It's making her want to give Lina up for adoption," Adam added icily.

I looked down. I knew she was looking at me, waiting for me to deny what Adam had said, but I couldn't because it was true.

Silence.

"How could you? How could you say such a thing?" my mom's voice came exploding at me. "All this time I've been wondering what's wrong with you. How come you're not happy? And now you say this. How could I possibly have a daughter like you? How could my daughter be so cruel?" She was shaking her head and looked utterly distraught.

I was stunned by her words. Yes, it was true that I was always weepy and sad. But I was a good mom, feeding my baby at all hours, loving her despite the strange, pervasive grief within me. And most importantly, when I saw that terrifying image of what I might do to her, I wanted to protect her.

I sat there in silence, contemplating what had just transpired. The fullness in my breasts returned and I held out my arms, indicating I wanted Lina. Grudgingly, she was handed to me, and I mechanically latched her to my breast. My mom sat across from me supervising, tears rolling down her face.

· · ·

"So here it is!" Adam said, dangling a drugstore bag in his hand about half an hour later. He yanked the bag off the pump and presented it to me. He was back to his old good-natured self.

"Come on, let's try it out!"

He sounded so excited that I unlatched Lina. I followed the instructions he got from the pharmacist about sticking my nipple into the funnel and then squeezing the trigger, or whatever it was called. It was a simple old-fashioned bare-bones pump. Nothing happened. After twenty minutes I gave up. We decided breastfeeding was easier.

· · ·

"Come upstairs," my mom would say, every hour that I was in the basement alone with Lina. Adam had gone back to work after taking three weeks off.

"Why don't you sleep with Lina in the same bed? It'll bring you two closer together. Try it and you'll see."

Suggestions kept creeping up from different people: my mom, dad, Adam.

"Why don't you cuddle her?"

"Why don't you give her a bath, instead of Adam doing it all the time?"

"Why don't you go for a walk to make yourself feel good?"

Sometimes they came when we were chatting, sometimes when we were chopping vegetables, and sometimes when we were sipping tea. Advice even came via a phone call from my sister in Buffalo.

> *Soft pulsating fontanel. Long iron handrail. The soft top of her fragile skull colliding with the edge, the unusually pointy edge of the handrail along our basement stairs. Blood pouring out of the jagged puncture wound.*

This refrain kept intruding in my mind whenever I least expected it. I could be doing my nails or even bathing when it would come and paralyze me. The only thing it made me confident of was that I couldn't trust myself to sleep with Lina, to cuddle her, or be too close with her, lest I accidentally act on the gruesome imagery appearing in my head.

• • •

"Mom, I think you're right." I said, rounding the corner into the kitchen one morning.

"About what?" she said, looking over at me from where she stood cutting up chicken at the sink. Why she just didn't buy pre-cut pieces was one thing I'd never understand. For the longest time, I thought that chicken didn't come pre-cut because I'd always seen my mom do it herself.

"About going out to get some fresh air. It can't hurt, right?" As the days passed, I was sounding more and more like my old self, even if I wasn't feeling like it. To be honest, the melancholy had improved. It was just my other symptom — the recurring violent imagery — that was a problem.

"Exactly! Now don't forget to bundle Lina up properly before you go," she said, smiling.

"Why?" I asked.

"Because it's chilly out!"

"Right," I said uncomfortably.

I hadn't planned on going out with Lina. Getting away from Lina was why I *needed*, not wanted, to get out for a bit. Everything I did for Lina, whether it was putting her to sleep, giving her a bath, or carrying her around, was a trigger for brutal images: her tiny face submerged in the bathwater, a piece of my clothing blocking her attempts to breathe, her newborn body flying down the staircase and lying crumpled on the floor. Nothing I did could stem the flow, and I was frightened.

"Mom?"

"Yes, honey?" she said, having moved on to wiping the counters. She was always in motion, doing something.

"I was thinking that maybe this time I would go out on my own. You know, I could walk really fast and get the blood flowing," I said, fiddling with the tablecloth.

"Why would you want to do that when you can go with this little cutie?" she said. My mom slipped past me and was now hovering over Lina, who was kicking up a storm, excited by the sudden attention she was eliciting from grandma. Her kicking was so fierce that she even toppled over the fortress of pillows I had surrounded her with to make sure she wouldn't fall off the edge of the sofa.

"Yeah well, you know …" I didn't finish.

"Listen. You have to take Lina. You can't leave her here with me, if that's what you're thinking. She's got to be with her mom now, not her grandma. Okay? I'll get her dressed; you go and get yourself ready."

I could have easily debated the point, but at that moment I felt I couldn't. I needed to get someone on my side. Adam. I dialed him up at work.

"Adam, hope I'm not bothering you. I just wanted to surprise you and let you know that I'm taking your suggestion and am going out for a walk."

"Hey, that's great. You'll feel awesome," he said. I could tell he was grinning.

"But can you believe my mom is saying I should take Lina?" I said, feigning incredulity. I figured he'd take the bait and support me.

"I think she's right," he said, to my surprise. "You *should* go out with Lina. Actually, make sure you take her with you, okay? Don't just leave her with your mom, all right?"

As I hung up the phone, it suddenly hit me why both my mom and Adam wanted me to take Lina. It was obvious. They too were experiencing the violent thoughts and images in *my* head and couldn't trust themselves to be alone with her.

I dressed quickly and ran upstairs to grab Lina out of my mom's arms. Of course I would take Lina with me. I was her mother, and it was my responsibility to protect her. Especially now, since my family was clearly admitting that they were capable of giving in to the violent images that danced around in *my* head.

We went on lots of long walks after that, almost daily. Every afternoon, I would yank open her stroller, the one Adam swore required a college degree to operate. Once, far from home, Adam and I had even forgotten how to close it before putting it in the car. After almost an hour of taking turns holding Lina while the other parent tried to figure out how to close the stroller, we almost gave up and abandoned it right there and then.

"What's the big deal? We'll just buy another one. Forget it," Adam had said, just as I yanked the little plastic piece on the side. The stroller finally snapped shut, as though frightened by the very prospect of being abandoned.

The same stroller now crunched over fallen twigs and tiny pieces of gravel as we walked. The sun beat down on Lina as we trudged along, taking in the beautiful summer weather. I kept stopping to adjust the retractable canopy, trying to make sure she was getting enough light, but not too much. She was still so little and needed to be facing me while we walked. This was all the better for me, as it allowed me to keep a close watch, see her cuteness in all its glory, and witness her experiencing the world.

I knew young babies couldn't see far or really smile out of joy. But her occasional gurgles made me feel like she really was enjoying the leaves dancing in the breeze or the wind tickling her face. It felt good to take Lina for a walk, even if it was because I couldn't trust anyone to not act on the violence playing out in my head.

. . .

Soft pulsating fontanel. Long iron handrail. The soft top of her fragile skull colliding with the edge, the unusually pointy edge of the handrail along our basement stairs. Blood pouring out of the jagged puncture wound.

Standing in the shower, I covered my face with my hands as the hot water rained down on me. I couldn't understand why the image kept materializing at random, invading my consciousness like an intruder. Worse was that I had no weapons to stop the invasion.

Why did it keep coming? The scalding water felt good on my body, a stark contrast to how the image in my mind made me feel. I shifted around in the shower, letting the water envelop me.

The haunting image sat frozen on the canvas in my mind.

Interesting. Very interesting.

It felt like I was hearing myself think.

Exactly how much pressure did it take for that hand-rail to pierce the fontanel?
Would the handle of a broom work?
How about a butter knife?

The questions felt intriguing, like they were part of a scientific inquiry. The answers to these questions were important, even necessary. The quest to answer them felt strangely compelling. Though still unwanted, the image no longer produced the old sick feeling.

· · ·

"Bye Mom, bye Dad," I said, leaning in to give my father another hug. We were standing in the foyer by the front door, where all the shoes sat neatly lined up beneath the shoe-shaped sign that read "Take yours off!"

I was pretty sure it was the sixth time I was saying my goodbyes. My mom stood holding Lina, and tears were rolling down both my parents' faces. Loud sniffles punctuated the sound of them smothering Lina with kisses. I could see the beginning of a smile creeping onto Adam's face, and I felt the strong urge to kick him.

So what if he was right, that we were only going ten minutes away, back to our own home? My parents were justified in feeling sad. We had been living in their basement for the past two and half months, one month longer than initially planned. They were used to having unfettered access to their granddaughter at all hours of the day. This meant they were truly going to miss her.

Even though we had been initially forced to stay there by my mom, it was now because of her gentle nudging that we were finally leaving. "I think it's time you and Adam thought of going back home," she had announced, a couple of evenings earlier.

I had come up from the basement to get Lina from my parents so they could have their evening cup of tea. I sat nursing Lina on the overstuffed armchair across from them as they explained.

"You're doing so much better now," my mom said, placing her mug beside her on the table. "Lina needs a proper routine, and that needs to start at your house. You need to get her used to sleeping in her crib in her own room."

"Yes," my dad added. "Your mom, she knows these things. Look at what a great job she did with you guys. It wasn't me. It's all thanks to your mom."

They were each other's biggest fans, and they made no bones about it. It was true, my mom did do a lot of the heavy lifting, but my dad was not the slouch he painted himself as. His hands were just as dirty, not only with diapers, but by turning us into avid readers and writers.

I nodded at everything they said. I didn't want to leave their home and would have been happy staying longer, but I knew what they were saying was right. Not only that, but Adam would be ecstatic.

I caught sight of Adam's face as he burst out laughing. "Come on, Mom, Dad; we're just ten minutes away."

I gave him a furious, pleading look. I wanted him to stop laughing. He didn't care. Taking Lina from my mom, he started strapping her into the car seat.

"And the way you drive, Dad, speeding without checking blind spots, you can be there in four, maybe five minutes tops," he said, teasingly.

I shook my head, embarrassed on behalf of my parents.

As our car turned into the familiar entrance of our gray stone building, I leaned over Lina, clutched her tiny hand and whispered, "Welcome home."

6: PLAYING THE FOOL

Soft pulsating fontanel. Long iron handrail. The soft top of her fragile skull colliding with the edge, the unusually pointy edge of the handrail along our basement stairs. Blood pouring out of the jagged puncture wound.

THE IMAGES KEPT COMING, BUT NOW THERE WAS NO nausea or disgust. The scientific interest was gone too. Now, I had no reaction.

I sucked in my cheeks to highlight where I needed to dab a bit of blush. Gone were the printed postpartum granny gowns I used to live in at my mom's. All my life, I'd heard how important it was to get yourself out of your jammies and look the part if you wanted to change how you felt. Hence, these days I'd wake up, shake out my curls, add some lipstick, and sometimes even layer on eyeliner by midmorning.

I was grateful to still be off work. Adam and I had decided before Lina was born that I would stay home until the baby was at least a year old. Nevertheless, I brought routine into my day:

sleeping in a bit, tidying up, spending quality time with Lina in the form of walks around the neighbourhood, cooking dinner, and then waiting for Adam to come home. The melancholy from the weeks prior had reduced significantly, but it had been replaced with a gnawing feeling within me, one that I couldn't quite place.

The wheels of Lina's stroller crunched the twigs and seeds beneath it. My neighbourhood was very different from my mom's. A lot more trees meant more acorns, and tiny mountains of winged seeds lay scattered about. The smell of freshly mown grass filled my nostrils as I crossed the street, heading toward the shortcut to the park. Lina was too little to play, but it was still a nice place to sit and chat. I stationed myself on a bench beneath a large tree with a huge canopy of leaves.

"So what's going on?" I asked, looking her right in the eye.

She gurgled back, happy for the attention.

"No really," I said. "Why are you taking up all my time? Can't you see I'm exhausted?"

She blew a raspberry at me.

I smiled, straightening up. That was so adorable. Enough chit-chat, I decided. We headed back home.

• • •

I rocked Lina in my arms as I stood in the living room. She was splayed on her side, her belly up against my own. This technique seemed to work for Adam whenever she had colic. But the screaming continued. I paced, rocking her from side to side. I'd do whatever was necessary to get her to stop.

The gnawing feeling had been growing slowly over the past several days. Now it was a fully formed thought.

She's doing it on purpose!

I looked down at her aghast. Could it be true? I rushed down the hall, laying her down in her crib even though she was still crying. I flicked on the baby monitor and went for a long hot shower.

• • •

She's doing it on purpose!
She's doing it on purpose!

It popped up whenever she became colicky or cried because she couldn't sleep.

She's doing it on purpose!
She's doing it on purpose!

"She's not like this at all when she's with me," I said to Adam when I saw him console Lina or skillfully put her to sleep. Everything she did, from trying to match the movements of her mouth to his, to cooing and echoing the sounds he was making at her, was so *infantile*. I was dumbstruck at how much she resembled a baby with him and increasingly resentful at the obvious split in her personality and behaviour toward me.

Back and forth I glided in the nursing chair in my room. I could hear the clicking sound of Lina nursing as I sat, contemplating what she was doing to me. What were her motivations? Did she want Adam to leave me, or me to leave Adam? What did she gain by driving a wedge between us?

The clicking continued, as though she was unaware of what was unfolding in my mind.

I needed to ask her. There was no way I was going to be able to figure out what she was plotting, because she was so adept at concealing things. Look at how she was making me seem like a fool right now!

The clicking slowed, and I saw her trying to pull away from me. Her head lolled about as I sat her up. She was in a drunken stupor. One eye looked at me lazily, while the other was already closed.

Sorry, she was going to have to answer, no matter how tired she was, or at least was pretending to be. I balanced her carefully on one arm of the glider and made sure we were facing each other properly. "What is it that you want?" I asked. She was more awake now, after the forced activity.

Slow blink. Yawn.

"Are you going to tell me or not?"

The blinking continued, and she tried to touch my mouth with her tiny hand.

"Don't look at me like that, okay," I said, anger rising in me. Why was she taunting me like this, acting like she was a baby, when we both knew she wasn't? "Just tell me what you want, you idiot!" I screamed into her face, restraining the intense urge to give her a shake and force her to tell me.

Lina's bottom lip began to tremble and slowly push forward. She closed her eyes and wailed with intense sadness.

I looked at her and felt wicked. I lay her down in her crib, turned on the baby monitor, and went for another long hot shower.

• • •

"Let's show Daddy what you're all about, young lady," I said, zooming into Lina's crying face. She was lying in her playpen, fiercely screaming at the injustice of being forced to lie in it. I was so happy we had bought a new video camera. After the screaming session of the other day, I'd vowed to stop interrogating her. But with the camera, I could document her behaviour for all to see.

60

"She's been like this for forty minutes and nothing I do is making her stop," I said, into the microphone in a monotone. The phone started ringing mid-recording. I hit pause and went to grab it.

"Hey, Aaisha. How's everything? We haven't spoken in so long," my sister, Mariya, said.

I tried to remember how long it had been since we last talked. I couldn't, but it made sense, as we both had babies, and she also had a toddler to contend with.

"Oh, hey, yeah. Just been busy," I said truthfully.

"So, how are you feeling now?" she asked.

"Better. I'm not as sad anymore," I said. "It's just crazy hectic now. I don't know if Mom told you or what," I said, hesitating, wondering if I should confide in her what had been happening. "But I don't know what's wrong with Lina. Like she's always crying, never sleeps. It's unreal. What do you think I should do about her?"

"I'm not sure what you're saying, Aaisha. Babies are like that; they cry when they need comforting, and they cry when they're tired. It's normal."

"But not like her. She's not like a regular baby," I said.

"Everything you are saying is a normal part of motherhood. Why are you pathologizing your baby?" Mariya asked, bewildered.

"I'm not," I said, feeling unheard and dejected.

"Well, maybe you and I are just different types of moms then," she said.

The way she was raising her kids, she was the epitome of the mother I wanted to be. I felt sucker-punched by her words.

• • •

"Maybe I'll take Taboo," I suggested, peeking into the hallway closet. It was stuffed with everything and anything I didn't have a place for in the rest of our condo.

"Good idea!" Adam shouted back from where he was harnessing Lina into her car seat. We were headed to my mom's for a family dinner, and both my siblings and their families would be there.

Taboo was a family favourite and always made for hilarity. I loved how the better your grasp of the English language, the easier it was to describe the key word to your partner, without accidentally using one of the listed taboo words. Mariya and I were masters of the game, but not because of our superior vocabulary. We had a secret trick to winning almost each and every round: refer to shared life experiences to get your partner to say the key word.

"We all think Bill looks like one," I said, not even bothering to look at the list of taboo words I was to avoid.

"Refrigerator!" shouted my sister. All eyes were fixated on this dream team.

"Noreen's son Zaki has this," I said.

"Autism!" yelled my sister.

Beep. Beep. Beep. Time Over.

"Wowza!" I exclaimed, "We're on fire," I said, whipping down all the cards we'd won with.

"You guys are cheating!" yelled Adam, sitting up. We were all sprawled on my mom's living room floor.

"How's that?" I countered.

"You two are drawing on stuff only you know about!"

"Who says you can't do that?" I challenged him, getting up on my knees. "Only sore losers!" I laughed triumphantly, high-fiving Mariya and collapsing backward with exaggerated affect. We'd won that round fair and square.

"Hey, on the topic of autism, I just read something in the paper about it. There was some study that said if your second toe is longer than your big toe, you have a greater chance of having a kid with autism," said Hannah, my brother's wife.

Second toe longer than big toe = autism

It burst into my mind immediately. That totally explained everything about Lina that I was having trouble with. It explained all the infantile behaviour: endless crying, inability to soothe herself and, worst of all, put herself to sleep.

"What's wrong? It's like you're not even playing," Mariya said.

She was right. This turn, I was busy scanning Adam's toes.

"Clouds? Sky? Airplane?" I shouted half-heartedly. Meanwhile, I managed a few glimpses: his second toe was not longer. Perhaps Hannah had misread the article? Maybe she mixed up toes for fingers?

· · ·

"Well that was a fun evening," Adam said. He pulled back the sheets on our bed and climbed in.

I nestled in beside him.

"Let's compare hand sizes; I've gained ten pounds, so maybe my hands have grown bigger," I said. He'd never suspect my motivation, since this was something we often did to marvel at the crazy difference in our sizes. We touched, palm to palm. His middle finger was long. Really long.

"Man, you're tiny! You sure you're not some sort of dwarf?" he said, laughing. He pulled out the pillow from behind his head and flung it across the floor before lying down.

I lay down too. I couldn't get the image of his unnaturally long middle finger out of my head. Worse, I couldn't get the idea of what it meant out of my head: Lina was autistic. I felt sad, but strangely excited. Saddened at her diagnosis, but excited to finally know what was going on.

1:30 a.m.

1:52 a.m.

1:58 a.m.

The numbers on the clock changed slowly, mocking me, reminding me that a watched clock never ticks.

2:05 a.m. I sat up, fed up with waiting.

"Adam."

"Adam."

"*Adam*," I said, shaking him, a sense of urgency in my voice. "Wake up honey. Sometimes things happen that we're not prepared for. Maybe it's better like this," I said, seeing him sit up and fumble around on the table for his glasses.

"What? What are you talking about? What happened?" he asked. Shoving his glasses onto his face, he peered at me through the slice of moonlight coming from between the blinds.

"It's always better to find out earlier than later. This way we can do something about it." How to lighten the blow? I knew, having been a psych major, that autism wasn't a death sentence, but he wouldn't know that.

"Can you just spit it out? What the hell is going on?" he yelled, making me jump. Where did that angry outburst come from?

"She's autistic. Lina is autistic!" I shouted back, more because I was alarmed than because I was angry. "She's almost three months old, doesn't know how to soothe herself, cries for everything, can't put herself to sleep. It's not normal. I want to take her to the doctor," I said, shaking my head. "It's not developmentally appropriate."

Silence. Pulling off his glasses, he turned his back to me and went to sleep.

· · ·

We pulled in by the brownstone clinic. Even though the clinic was downtown, nearly an hour from our place in the suburbs, it was known to be the best place to find specialists who knew their stuff. It was closely aligned to the hospital next door and was also a teaching facility for doctors doing their residency.

My new doctor, the one I had switched to when I got pregnant with Lina, was on vacation. Fortunately, she was part of a practice that allowed you to see anyone on her team. They all had access to your notes, so it felt like whichever doctor you met still had a sense of who you were.

I pulled the unusually heavy glass door toward me, holding it open to allow Adam to pass through with Lina in the car seat.

"Remember, let's just lay out the facts, not editorialize, and let the doctor come to her own conclusion," I said. Silence. He must feel like his world has shattered, I concluded, feeling sorry for him.

The doctor would see for herself how infantile she was, incapable of doing anything, lacking in her ability to form bonds, which was why I couldn't soothe her or comfort her. Poor Lina. All this time she was autistic, rather than being purposefully incapable or two-faced. At least now the doctor would confirm it and all would be well.

A young Asian doctor stepped into the room. She smiled broadly. "Hi, my name's Dr. Nguyen," she said. She had square glasses and a short blunt haircut that framed her face neatly. She looked kind, and I sensed she would easily pick up on Lina's problem.

"Mommy's going to take off your little sleeper, so Dr. Nguyen can see how big and strong you are," I said to Lina as I took off her clothes. I turned to the doctor, offering up a diaper-clad Lina.

"You want this, don't you?" Dr. Nguyen teased, swinging her stethoscope at a wriggling Lina. Tiny reaching hands opened and closed eagerly at the sight of it. She gurgled excitedly. A smile settled on her chubby, cherub-like face as the doctor let her grasp hold of it.

"My wife thinks she's developmentally slow or delayed," Adam said uncomfortably.

"Her?" Dr. Nguyen asked, surprised. "Look at her. She's vocalizing, grasping, interested, and even smiling. She's as healthy as you're going to get them!"

I looked from Lina to the doctor, then back at Lina.

"But you, Mom," Dr. Nguyen said, zipping Lina back into her sleeper. "I think you should be going out to meet other moms and stuff, so that you don't start looking for things to worry about." I stiffened uncomfortably.

7: THE OTHER WOMAN

TIP #8: TO KEEP A BABY CALM, GIVE YOUR BABY A full body massage. I put aside my new parenting book.

Adam and Lina sat together in the nursing glider, clearly not nursing. He was holding her up, blowing raspberries at her. So that's where she'd learned her cutesy behaviour from!

"Excuse us," I said, taking Lina from Adam.

"Hey, why?" he said, making an exaggerated pouty face.

"You'll see," I said, taking off her clothes on my bed. "Can you get me the baby oil and change mat?"

Adam returned with both, and I lay Lina face-down on the mat. Squirming uncomfortably, she looked like a little brown worm. I put my oiled hands on her back, rubbing her down just the way it said to in the book. Her squirming lessened and I could hear small grunts of approval.

"I want to go to the mall and window shop like we used to, so I'm taking care of Lina's needs before we get to mine," I said, smiling up at Adam.

"Smart. When's my turn?" Adam quipped.

. . .

We turned into the busy parking lot. Everyone was out to enjoy the beautiful day. Almost right on cue, I heard the beginning of a whimper. But I'd just nursed her, changed her, and had even given her a full body massage. I started unbuckling Lina from her car seat as the fussing intensified. Maybe the fresh air would calm her down.

I paced outside the car, swinging her gently from side to side. The crying continued. I switched it up and started bouncing her up and down. She switched to screaming.

"Let me try," Adam said, reaching over to take her from me. The screaming continued. The intense summer heat wasn't helping.

I could feel my face falling at the prospect of not being able to go out and do something normal, something enjoyable.

"It's no use," Adam said. "I'll just take her home."

"No," I said, coming to try again with Lina.

"Look, I'll take her home so that you can go and window shop, okay?" Adam said earnestly.

"No, I'll get her to calm down," I said, rocking her.

"It's so hot out here, and she's just a baby," Adam protested.

You can't trust him. Don't let him take her.

I took in the thought.

"Aren't you going to give her to me?" he asked, arms outstretched.

You can't trust him. Don't let him take her.

I saw eagerness in Adam's face, like he really wanted me to give her to him. He looked *too* eager.

"We'll come back to get you," he said.

*He wants to take her home by himself, so he can have
his way with her!*

I stumbled back from his reaching arms with the newest
thought, repulsed, disgusted, frightened, and suddenly feeling protective of Lina. Horrified by what he wanted to do to our innocent
baby, I knew it was on me to keep her safe.

"No!" I screamed. "You can't take her."

Adam's face registered shock, then anger. "You're selfish and crazy,"
he said, grabbing Lina out of my arms and opening the back door.

My own face felt hot with anger. I went around the other side
and got in the middle seat, right beside Lina. I could see Adam fum-
bling with the straps as he tried to strap her in. He was muttering
and I could make out a few words: "selfish," "mall," and "crazy."

My mind was a jumble of confusing thoughts:

> *Adam must want to sexually assault Lina. He's a
> sick, sick man. I just want to have a normal life. I
> want to go to the mall. I am not selfish. I am pro-
> tecting Lina. He's a sick, sick man.*

Silently, we entered the highway, but my mind was anything but
silent. The jumble was still in my head.

> *Adam must want to sexually assault Lina. He's a
> sick, sick man. I just want to have a normal life. I
> want to go to the mall. I am not selfish. I am pro-
> tecting Lina. He's a sick, sick man.*

"What the hell?" I heard Adam shout as the car careened left.
His right arm was trying to stop the heavy blows to his head I was
delivering from the back seat.

He's a sick, sick man. He's a sick, sick man. He's a sick, sick man.

I kept feeling more energized with every iteration of the thought, which made me punch Adam more ferociously.

A hand suddenly gripped my face hard. It felt strong. Stronger than me, and it forced me reluctantly back into my seat.

I sat in my seat, strangely still. Tears sprang into my eyes with a sudden realization, and I tasted saltiness in my mouth. Adam, the love of my life, the one who had never laid a hand on me in all our years together, had just *abused* me.

"Let me out now!" I screamed, my breathing coming in a rush. The car was no longer veering this way and that way. "I want to get out of the car now!" I said, opening the door.

Adam's horrified face turned to look at me. His arm grabbed mine, the one I was using to open the door.

I could feel the wind pulling the door open wider. It was like the door agreed that I needed to get away from Adam. I grappled to control the door while also trying to wrestle myself away from Adam's grip. "I need to get out. I need to get out," I said pleadingly. His vice-like grip held me down, even though the car door was doing its best to let me escape.

"Let me pull over then; let me pull over," he repeated desperately.

I pulled the reluctant door shut. He stopped on a residential street, and I opened the door.

Adam reached over and gently held my hand. "I'm sorry, I didn't mean to hurt you," he said quietly.

I nodded and got out of the car.

My life was a mess: my family couldn't be trusted with Lina; she was autistic and then she wasn't; Adam wanted to sexually abuse her, and now he was a physical abuser as well. I loved Lina, but I couldn't protect her anymore. It was too much, and I was exhausted. I wanted a normal life, to be able to enjoy the simple things like going to the mall, reading a book, watching a movie. From now on, God would have to protect my little baby, because I was done.

I decided to go over to the plaza across from where Adam had dropped me. Signs boasting of the best jerk chicken in town and Tylenol on sale blasted at me from shop windows. If only my problems could be solved by a warm meal or a couple of painkillers. I went over to a convenience store emblazoned with an ATM logo and took out some money. I wanted to catch a bus and go somewhere, anywhere, away from my family.

I sat down on the grass near the bus stop. Ignorant of directions, I figured wherever the bus took me would be fine. Destination unknown worked for me.

Forty minutes. I'd been sitting, waiting in the suffocating heat for forty minutes. Where on earth was the damn bus? I got up and walked to the parking lot of the plaza. I could still see if the bus was coming, but maybe walking a little would help cool me down a bit. It was working. I felt less sticky.

Crying.

I heard crying from somewhere. Crying that sounded familiar: Lina. I looked around and caught sight of Adam parked near the plaza, jiggle-walking Lina up and down. She was inconsolable and I knew why. I walked over.

Mechanically, I took her from him. I sat on the curb of the parking lot, unbuttoned the top of my blouse and started nursing her. Lina settled quickly, and I could hear the familiar clicking sound. She began toying with my blouse and reached up to stroke my face innocently. Her wide, dark eyes looked up at me. How could I abandon such an adorable face? As I buttoned up my top, I decided I would leave another day.

PART 2

• • •

June 20, 2001: "Mom Drowns 5 Children in Texas."

That headline was plastered across every newspaper in the United States. Adam and I had driven down to visit Mariya and her family in Buffalo for the week. One of our days coincided with Mariya's best friend Sue's visit.

I was pushing Lina's stroller through the crowded mall. This huge space was nothing like the malls I was used to back home. It was like everyone was on one of those crazy shopping sprees I'd always dreamed of winning as a teen. People milled about everywhere, and I was trying hard to focus on not hitting anyone.

"How could a mother ever do that to her children?" Sue mused loudly, catching sight of the headlines as we passed by a Smoker's Corner–type convenience shop.

"I can see why she would do it," I said. I thought about how brave that mom was to send her kids so lovingly to Heaven, away from this perilous world.

Mariya was on her cell phone co-ordinating where we would meet up with the men, so I didn't get her take on the matter. She didn't hear what I said, but Sue did. As we caught up with Adam and the others, I caught the horrified look on her face.

• • •

Buffalo had been fun, but the real highlight of the summer was a getaway to Niagara Falls for Adam, Lina, and me. Though it was way beyond our meager budget, we managed to spend a few days at a four-star hotel near the falls. The falls were supposed to be an awe-inspiring testament to the power of nature, something to make us reflect on the beauty surrounding us. Scenic walks, lots of cuddling, and lots of pictures were on the agenda.

"Back, back, back," Adam said, trying to capture the perfect picture of Lina and me alone together. I was frozen about two metres in front of the metal fence before the falls. "How come you're not moving back? This is going to make for a weird picture."

"I don't want to," I said. "Just take it like this. I'd rather have a picture with her on the grass."

"Fine," he said, snapping a quick picture that he clearly didn't approve of.

I sat down on the grass, relieved to be away from the rampaging water. The water gripped me with intense fear that I might suddenly jump in or worse, toss Lina into the cold. I held Lina up, pressed her cheek against my own, and smiled.

Click. "Beautiful," Adam announced.

• • •

Adam was in love with a large, beautiful woman from work.

I felt stunned by what I had learned from my dream, which felt more like a nightmare. I was not even a hundred pounds, so it cut me like the ultimate betrayal. *She* stood six feet tall and had a baby of her own. In the dream, he had helped her with her baby stroller down the stairs of a ridiculously tall building but wouldn't help me.

"Why are you doing this to me?" I wept.

"Because she has so much juicy flesh compared to you," he replied, licking his lips and lustfully giving her meaty hips a pinch. She looked over at me, flipped her hair, and smiled.

I woke, distraught, and determined to put an end to their love affair.

Pacing about my home, I kept checking the clock. I needed to wait for the right time to call. Ten fifteen seemed about right; it would be time for his break.

"Hello?" I listened carefully. Maybe I could hear her in the background.

"Aaisha!" Adam said, acting like he was genuinely happy to hear my voice. It sounded real, but I knew it was a ploy. "How are you and Lina doing?" he asked. Like he really cared.

"Fine," I said. "We're both fine. She's playing in her bouncy chair."

I looked over to where she was trying to use her little fingers like pincers, grabbing at one of the dangly toys hanging in front of her. "So, who's with you right now?" I asked, trying to sound nonchalant.

"No one but me," he said perplexed.

"No one? You sure?"

"No one that I can see." From the way his voice sounded, it seemed like he was moving his head from side to side to check. But I knew it was just a ruse to throw me off.

"Okay, nothing new on my side," I said. "See you soon." I hung up. Maybe she was on her break somewhere else. I'd try again later.

I dialed him up again fifteen minutes later. "Hello?" I said. "Me again, hon. How are you?"

"Great," he said. "And you?"

"Good. I know I just called, but I wanted to hear your voice again, 'cause I missed you!"

"I miss you too, honey."

Laughter. I heard a distinctly female laugh from where he was. It sounded really close, too close.

"Who's that?" I asked, not sounding so nonchalant. My antenna was up, way up.

"What do you mean?" he asked, seemingly confused.

"That person laughing. Who is it?"

"That's just Wendy. She sits next to me," he said, laughing.

I heard muffled speech, like Adam was covering the mouthpiece and talking to someone. I felt a shiver run through my body.

"I gotta go," he said abruptly, before hanging up.

I paced my living room contemplating it all. Her name was Wendy, she sat near him, and he preferred her over me.

Every day, as I went by my daily routines of nursing Lina, taking her on walks around the neighbourhood, and giving her a bath, my mind ran through various scenarios of Adam's interactions with Wendy.

Him sitting on her desk telling jokes.
Her sitting on his desk, flipping her long hair this
way and that.

Unwilling to give up on Adam so easily, I peppered him with multiple calls a day for the next few weeks.

Him offering her the lunch I made.

The audacity of it all! I was furious. Shouldn't he be working instead of spending all his time at work with Wendy? Bent on getting him back to his own desk, I called. "Hi honey."

"Hey," he said, breathing hard. He was breathing hard because he'd just come running over from Wendy's desk, no doubt. "Can't talk now, gotta go," he said abruptly, before hanging up. I was livid and sad.

"Hey family," he said, stepping into our home later that evening. His face looked worn and tired. Shouldn't that be how *I* looked, considering all he was putting me through? Still, I gave him a hug and we settled on the couch together.

"I guess I have to tell you at some point," he said.

Worry gripped me. What was he going to tell me? The list of possible confessions was too great to contemplate.

He took a crumpled piece of paper from his pocket. "It's not looking good for me. Mary's asked for a meeting with me to discuss my job performance," he said, looking sad.

I decided against bringing up my concerns about Wendy.

8: THE INTERVENTION

"HOW COME YOU NEVER LET LINA COME OVER AND spend time with just me and your dad?" my mom asked, her voice sounding hurt.

My mother was nagging me again. She'd been calling and laying this guilt trip on me for the past couple of weeks. Adam's meeting about his poor performance at work was concerning enough without this being an issue too.

"I can't," I said exasperatedly. "She'll cry." It was the truth. She would cry, and maybe even get into one of her endless crying jags. Then my mother might shake her, beat her, or do some other awful thing to her, and then she'd be dead.

"Mariya was never like this," she said, her voice breaking.

"Yeah, well, I have to go," I said, hanging up.

• • •

"Listen, your folks told me they wanna come over and talk about a few things," Adam said the following Saturday.

I couldn't believe my parents were involving Adam in this. "My gosh. It's that whole 'why can't Lina stay with us?' issue again," I said, rolling my eyes.

"So are you game?" he asked.

I felt angry but didn't want to seem like the bad guy. "Fine," I said. "But I want you to mediate."

We hurried around, tidying the house and getting Lina ready, but she fell asleep before they arrived.

When we heard them knock, Adam went to open the door and let them in. I was surprised to see my dad, mom, Mariya, and my brother, Idris.

They gathered in our crowded living room. It'd never seemed so small before. My dad and Idris sat on the sofa together, while my mom and Mariya were together on the chaise diagonal from them. Adam sat in the relic, the '70s-style chair. I positioned myself opposite him in a dining chair.

"So, how should we start?" Adam asked, assuming his mediator role right off the bat. Everyone sat strangely silent for a family full of big mouths. I saw my mom looking down.

"Well, they're our guests, so I guess they should start," I said, trying to break the silence.

"Why don't you ever hug or kiss Lina? It's almost like you don't like her. And it's *so* unlike you."

"You get so mad whenever anyone mentions co-sleeping with Lina. Where are your maternal instincts?"

"You're such a hugger, but you never give her hugs. Why?"

"You're not acting like a mom. How come?"

"The way you keep her away from us, it looks like you don't want anyone to love her. Why?"

The list of complaints about me was vast and varied. I could see Adam frowning and trying to keep up while taking notes. I felt my face getting hotter with each new complaint. They were trying to paint a picture of me as a bad mom. It was something I knew couldn't be further from the truth.

Despite the anger rising in me, I sat quietly, letting them get it all out. Adam nodded his head at me once he'd finished jotting it all down.

"Listen," I said. "I know what you are all doing." I saw puzzled glances being exchanged between them.

"You're trying to make it look like I hate Lina," I continued, my voice beginning to shake with anger. The puzzled expressions stayed put. "But I know it's really all of *you* that hate Lina!" I announced, jumping to my feet.

All of their eyebrows rose in astonishment.

"Don't try to deny it," I yelled. "I've known for a long while now," I said, surveying them defiantly. My heart was beating rapidly in my chest.

"Even when she was having colic, you all acted like she didn't have it because you didn't want to admit it. Because if you did admit it, it would be like admitting you hate her."

I saw everyone's jaw drop, even Adam's. It was evident that they had thought I didn't know.

I whipped around to my mother. "And you, you can't even trust yourself to be alone with Lina," I said, shaking my head in disgust. It felt good to let it all out and let them know that I knew.

Looking at me incredulously, she shook her head at me, pretending to disagree. But I wasn't about to let her get away with her charade any longer.

"Isn't that why you yourself told me the very first time I wanted to go for a walk by myself that I *had* to take Lina? You wanted me to take her because you couldn't trust yourself with her!" I said triumphantly.

I had so deftly defeated all their points that Adam wasn't bothering to take notes anymore. I sat down to silence. Then the silence was suddenly penetrated by soft chuckles.

"What on earth are you saying? Are you even *listening* to yourself?" Idris said, breaking into hysterics.

Laughter rose all around me. I thought I even heard Adam laughing, albeit uncomfortably. Nobody said anything else, but the laughter kept getting louder.

I felt my face getting hot again, and I felt dizzy. "Get out of my house," I said, breathing hard. "Get out of my house," I repeated, rising to my feet.

The laughter began fading, and I saw confused looks being exchanged.

"GET OUT OF MY HOUSE, NOW!" I yelled at the top of my lungs. My fists were balled up, ready to let fly. Adam was on his feet, trying to hold me, calm me down, fold me into him, but I was too riled up. "Make them leave, make them leave right now!"

Mouths agape, they stared at me and then began shuffling to the door, trading startled looks among themselves. I followed them to where they were bent over, putting on their shoes. I was breathing hard, but my heart was pounding harder, waiting for them to get out.

Idris straightened himself up and looked over at me. With a slow smile, he pointed his index finger to his temple and made a spinning gesture.

"You are totally crazy," he said, before opening the door and walking out.

I froze. It felt like I was falling down a huge, never-ending spiral staircase.

Mariya was straightening herself up, having just put on her shoes. I motioned for her to follow me into the kitchen. I continued falling down the staircase; my mom's and Mariya's own words from earlier swirled around me as I plummeted:

> *Mariya was never like this. Maybe we're just*
> *different types of moms.*
> *Mariya was never like this. Maybe we're just*
> *different types of moms.*

*Mariya was never like this. Maybe we're just
different types of moms.*

My sister joined me in the kitchen, looking eager to hear what
I had to say, like she wanted to help. As if. I shoved her up against
the wall.

*Mariya was never like this. Maybe we're just
different types of moms.
Mariya was never like this. Maybe we're just
different types of moms.
Mariya was never like this. Maybe we're just
different types of moms.*

"This is all your fault," I whispered into her surprised face before slamming my fist into her gut. I ran and quickly shoved my
feet into my shoes.

"I hate you guys — *all* of you!" I screamed as I rushed past my
family.

. . .

I raced down my condo's flight of stairs and stumbled out of the
building, relieved to breathe in the fresh air. I knew they would try
to come after me; they were my family after all.

Realizing that I was standing in plain sight at the front entrance, I looked around frantically, needing somewhere to hide.
From the corner of my eye, I glimpsed the little wooden fence some
five metres away. It kept the building's garbage dumpsters out of
sight and was adjacent to the parking lot.

Nobody would look near the dumpsters, I figured, hurrying to
crouch behind the largest trash bin.

"Where did she go?"

"Can you see her?"

"Let's get in the car and look."

I heard their loud voices and watched as they passed into the visitors' lot, where they were parked. They were no longer visible from my vantage point but, still wanting to know exactly where they were, I began straining to see past the large metal bin. I leaned on it to increase my line of sight.

It lurched forward. Terror set in as I saw that a small red car was reversing toward it. They were going to collide! I ran to wedge myself between the bin and the car. Perhaps my body could stop or slow the bin's momentum, and I could save a life. Having reached the front of the bin, I saw that the car had safely moved on. I breathed a sigh of relief.

"*Aaisha!* Aaisha!" I heard Adam shout.

Through the slats of the wooden fence, I caught a glimpse of Adam's face looking around wildly as he shouted my name. He was right at the entrance of our building, clutching the handle of Lina's car seat in one hand. Lina sat inside without even a blanket for cover, looking around.

"Hey, you didn't buckle her in!" I shouted, springing out from behind the fence. I was aghast that he'd carried her down without taking the necessary safety precautions. I saw Adam spin around and catch sight of me. Realizing my mistake, I ran for it.

"Buckle her in," I shouted as I ran past him onto the pavement. I turned to see Adam bent over, strapping Lina in. I continued running down the sidewalk, not sure exactly where I was going.

"Aaisha, stop. Please, Aaisha. Stop!"

I could hear Adam shouting, and by the sound of his voice, I knew he wasn't far behind. Why didn't they all just leave me alone? I hated them, *all* of them, including Adam. He was supposed to play mediator, but he hadn't said a word to support me during their accusations. I was even sure that I'd seen him laugh with the rest of them.

I stopped at the tiny plaza near my home, exhausted. It looked like it consisted of a single convenience store, but tucked around the corner was an abandoned entryway leading to an empty office. Nobody would think to come here. With my back and head pressed against the abandoned door, I heaved and let loose the tears raging inside.

My life since giving birth was nothing like I had imagined it was going to be. I replayed those few short months of torture. My family hated Lina and was at risk of harming her, even though they were denying it. Lina was either doing things on purpose to bother me or was autistic. Adam was a sexual predator and a wife abuser and was having an affair.

I slowly dropped to the ground, floored by the weight of it all.

"Aaisha? Aaisha?" Adam's voice broke into my thoughts.

I got back up into a crouch, ready to take flight. I cast furtive glances around to see where he was. My eyebrows rose in alarm at what I saw: directly across from me was my parents' tan van, driven by Idris. I could see faces peering at me as though I was a circus sideshow spectacle. Raising myself up, I tried to play it cool, like I was just chilling. I scanned my nails, like I'd just come to this precise spot to examine them.

Panting. I heard panting and then saw Adam in front of me. He looked winded, and the car seat dangled from the crook of one of his arms. He placed it down, trying to catch his breath. From the corner of my eye, I saw the van slowly creep forward and then disappear out of sight. Lina sat staring at me, blinking occasionally, sucking on her middle two fingers.

Adam and I walked home in silence, one of his arms around my shoulders while the other carried a sleeping Lina in her car seat.

• • •

Adam took me to my GP, Dr. Menko, later that week. Dr. Menko was a woman with a compact athletic build that belied her real age. She had well-worn creases on her face, particularly around her mouth. It made sense, as she liked to smile and laugh a lot. Today her hair was a surprising shade of purple.

"I'm miserable," I said as she entered the room. "I'm exhausted. Lina's always crying, I can't ever console her, and she can't even put herself to sleep." I left out the family politics and Adam's vices; they were personal issues. She listened while doing the stethoscope trick with Lina. She elicited the exact same excitement from Lina as the other doctor had.

"Maybe she has colic," Dr. Menko said, continuing to examine Lina by moving her legs in a bicycling motion and pressing her stomach. "The good news is that babies that have colic are usually healthy in every other aspect."

I tried to feign a happy smile.

"You know, some even theorize that babies that have colic grow up to have incredibly high IQs. Something about them being overly in tune with and sensitive to things around them. So, who knows?" she concluded, wrapping up her examination. She flashed us a smile.

"But what about Aaisha, doc?" Adam piped in, taking Lina from Dr. Menko.

"Yes, you," she said, nodding sympathetically. Patting me on the knee, she looked me in the eyes. "Motherhood *is* hard, isn't it?"

I looked down, biting my bottom lip. It was *beyond* hard, I thought. It felt like torture.

"It'll get better. I promise," she said, getting to her feet. I doubted it.

We stopped at my mom's house on the way home. I plunked myself down on the sofa. Laughter and shrieks of delight drifted in as my nieces and nephews played with the adults in the backyard.

They were hosting an impromptu BBQ because Mariya was still in town with her family. I sat by myself, avoiding everyone. It felt like they were all tiptoeing around me.

We left soon after arriving.

"I want to move to Vancouver," I said, turning to look at Adam as we drove home. "It's the only way I can be happy again." I wanted a fresh start with Lina and him, away from my family. It was obvious they hated me, and I couldn't imagine living in the same province as them and being forced to see them regularly. It would remind me of all the madness that came out at our meeting.

"We can look into that," Adam said. "Nothing has to be off the table."

I felt grateful to have Adam's support.

• • •

"You need to eat something," Adam said, balancing a tray with toast and some orange juice on it.

I shook my head. I'd been in bed for several days, only getting up to use the bathroom and feed Lina. I drew the covers over me and went back to sleep.

Almost a week later, after eating a bite that Adam forced on me, I called him over. "I need to tell you something," I said, sitting up a bit.

"What is it?" he said, coming to sit by me on the bed.

"There's something wrong with me," I said. "There's something really wrong with me. I just want to die. All the time. I just want to die. Leave me at a mental hospital or something," I continued. "Because I just want to die."

I slumped back down, exhausted.

"What are you saying?" Adam said, his voice unsure. He wore an expression I had never before seen on his face.

I felt so physically and mentally exhausted that I couldn't explain, even if I had wanted to.

"Why are you saying this?" he asked, his voice breaking. I could feel his hands searching for mine under the covers. He found my hand.

"Please," he said, now crying. "Please don't say that. We love you." I heard him heaving. "Lina loves you. She needs you. I love you. I need you," his voice faltered.

I couldn't tell if his voice was faltering because he couldn't talk anymore or because I'd drifted off to sleep.

9: THE F-WORD

FROM AUGUST OF 2001 UNTIL EARLY SEPTEMBER, I can recall nothing.

"The second tower has just been hit — this is unbelievable."

The radio was blaring loudly, and I couldn't believe what I was hearing. I sat up, alarmed. Was this really happening? Had the World Trade Center in New York actually been hit by a plane?

I made a silent prayer for the victims. Then I dialed my mom. "Hello, Mom?" I said. "Can you believe what just happened? It's so sad." I recounted the devastating clips of people jumping from the towers to their deaths. We talked about it more, and before hanging up, she asked about Lina.

"She's great," I said, looking down at Lina as she tried to sit up and grab the phone from me.

"We'll pop by later for a visit," I said. "Love you."

As I contemplated the unspeakable tragedy that was happening miles away, I smothered Lina with kisses. I felt so grateful for life, my life. I had everything I wanted. A beautiful healthy baby, a loving husband that was entirely committed to me, and a family that loved us.

I was acutely aware that what I was feeling now was incredibly different from how I had felt for the past several months. I wondered what could possibly have been wrong with me to make me think and believe such disturbing things, especially about Adam.

All I knew about what had transpired that month was that Adam was unemployed. The rest was a mystery.

. . .

"Show me a kissy face," I said, holding a six-month-old Lina up to me as we sat in the glider. She sucked in both her cheeks obligingly and stared at me. I melted into laughter. I might as well just have asked for a fishy face. She undid her kissy face.

"Through the garden, no time for a bite, I like to jump and like to hop!" I read. I simultaneously jerked up my knees so Lina would feel like she was literally jumping like the bunny in her book. It was her all-time favourite book, and her shoulders shook with excitement as she anticipated every line where she knew she would be bounced. I could tell she loved how I brought her stories to life. I felt in awe of everything she was able to do and relished in being able to share in every moment of it.

Though everything was marvellous with me, I'd periodically recall some of the thoughts I'd experienced in those early months. This time I didn't feel scared, or interested, just disgusted. It felt shocking that I'd ever experienced such bizarre thoughts or that I had believed I might be capable of harming my child. I wished I could erase the memories of that disturbing time, but they were part of my history whether I wanted to acknowledge them or not.

. . .

For the most part, nobody really discussed my transformation from Jekyll to Hyde, but it would sometimes creep up in the most insidious ways. Every time I wrapped up a visit to my parents, as I would get ready to leave, my dad would come to the door.

"Remember darling," he'd say. "Love your baby."

"I *do* love her," I'd say, sounding hurt, because that's how I truly felt.

"I know," he'd say, getting worried at my reaction. "I'm just saying. *You* are our baby and look at how much we love you!"

His words cut through me like a blade. And it didn't help that he'd say it every time we got together. After hearing it, I would always go home and spend an inordinate amount of time in the washroom, quietly weeping. It hurt that the people I loved and respected thought there had been a point in my life when I didn't love my daughter.

When Lina got a little older and had a pretty sophisticated understanding of language, my dad would still say it. However, aware of how smart she was, he switched to coming up to me and whispering it in my ear, as though it was our little secret. He thought it was something I needed to be reminded of on a regular basis, lest I forget and transition back to that old, unloving mother.

By that point, however, I'd long given up on protesting or arguing back and would just nod my head, accepting his sincere fatherly advice. I couldn't argue or say pretty much anything in response, because I understood where he was coming from. I recalled only too well the things I had said, thought, and believed in those early days, so how could I blame him or anyone else for remembering how I had behaved?

Though I knew my actions then had been a direct result of what was happening in my head, I still had no answer as to why I had experienced those things.

• • •

"Remember dear, love your baby," my dad whispered, for what was likely the five hundredth time since I had emerged from my personal hell.

I gave him my rehearsed nod. "Bye," I said, closing the door behind them.

They had just dropped by for a short visit with some homemade treats. Instead of feeling delighted, I felt saddened by his words — again. I had long promised myself to leave the matter to God. I reasoned that if there was someone who knew intimately what was up with me during those early months, it was God. And it was God, I figured, that would bring clarity to why I had acted the way I did.

Even though I made that promise to myself, I was only human, and the situation still pained me. I sat down in the tiny office I'd turned my hallway closet into. With Lina napping, I figured this was an opportune time to do some research.

Settling into my chair, I opened a Google tab. I typed: "Sadness after birth." I was surprised at how many entries popped up; there were tons. I clicked on one that sounded legit and started reading.

> Postpartum Depression (PPD) is a serious mood disorder. Women who develop PPD have feelings of intense sadness, worry, and exhaustion following childbirth. PPD is extremely common. Approximately one in seven can expect to experience depression in the year following childbirth. Fortunately, this disorder is treatable.

I swivelled around in my seat, intrigued. I read more. I kept swivelling. Was this what explained those first few torturous months of Lina's life? Some of it matched how I'd felt, but some didn't.

I swivelled some more, wondering why I had never been told about the possibility of developing this condition after giving birth.

Instead, all I remembered was being repeatedly instructed to check my legs for blood clots. Also, if this was a real medical thing, why hadn't Dr. Menko bothered to mention it, even after I told her how miserable I was?

My little internet foray taught me that I'd likely experienced postpartum depression in those first few months after Lina was born. Although serious bouts require medication, I appeared to have spontaneously recovered on my own. *Postpartum depression.* What I'd experienced in those early months finally had a name. Satisfied, I closed my open tabs and logged off.

. . .

Postpartum mood disorders are a significant global health concern. This is because when poor maternal mental health is left untreated, it not only negatively impacts a mother but also her child(ren) and the rest of her family. This spectrum of disorders includes postpartum depression, postpartum anxiety, postpartum obsessive-compulsive disorder, postpartum post-traumatic stress disorder, and at the most extreme, postpartum psychosis. Suicide is also a leading cause of maternal death in the postpartum period.

These illnesses have been found to exist in all races and across all cultures.[1] Despite the fact that they are a universal problem, they have a higher incidence among women of colour.[2] No one should be blamed for not knowing this or for being surprised by this, considering a cursory internet search of the topic features images of white women almost exclusively. Even white *men* feature more often in stock images of postpartum depression on the internet than racialized women.

Yet, in a study referenced by the Center for American Progress, the rate of postpartum mood disorders in women of colour is a striking 38 percent, as compared to the rate amongst all women, which is between 13 and 19 percent.[3] I have no doubt that failing to acknowledge this higher risk among racialized women plays a role in many of the other problems women of colour experience when it comes to postpartum mood disorders.

• • •

"Okay, I think it's time now," I said.

Lina peeled away from me. "Noooooooooo," she screamed, sprinting down the hallway to her room. I followed. I had waited long enough. She was three years old and could read every single picture book on her shelf and was at the point where she would correct me when I skipped over sentences in her *Peter Rabbit* books. Were those really designed to be read to children?

"You'll love it," I said. I had been trying to convince her to move on to chapter books so we wouldn't have to go to the library every two days. I was pretty sure she'd read all the picture books at the library already. Worse was that, even if we took out ten of them, she'd finish three on the drive back. I was at my wits' end.

She sat on her beanbag chair with the dreaded *Peter Rabbit* book in her hand. I was beginning to have a serious hate-on for Beatrix Potter.

"Look." I shook a copy of the Magic Treehouse book *Mummies in the Morning* at her.

She looked over at me, a gleam in her eye. I knew she wouldn't be able to resist. "I don't like books without pictures," she said.

"But there *are* pictures," I said, turning to a page with a black and white illustration.

"But I want lots of pictures."

"Of course; everyone likes lots of pictures."

She looked up, interested.

"Chapter books have lots of pictures too; I'll show you."

We sat down together on the sofa. "See, the pictures for these books are made in our head. We can see it when we close our eyes." She looked skeptical. "Let me show you: close your eyes." I started reading. A few minutes later, I paused.

"I want to keep reading, mama." There was an urgency in her voice. "My heart is going so fast," she said wild-eyed. She took the book and continued reading.

· · ·

As her appetite for chapter books grew, I began to carefully vet what she would select from the library. Adam and I even took the step of going through her books and crossing out all the offensive words that we thought a four-year-old shouldn't read.

As Adam and I sat in the living room watching *Lord of the Rings*, Lina came running from her room, her mass of curls bobbing up and down.

"Daddy, Mommy," she said, breathless. We hit pause.

"What is it, sweetheart?" I asked.

"Garfield's using the F-word," she said.

Adam and I exchanged surprised looks. I knew Garfield was an adult cat; it was easy to tell from his bored, middle-aged voice in the television cartoons, but for him to use the F-word was unexpected. I also couldn't figure out how Lina knew about the F-word; it wasn't like Adam or me to swear, especially in front of her.

I gulped. We would deal with that issue later.

I saw that her copy of *Garfield* was splayed open in one hand, while a stubby finger from the other hand strategically covered a word in the middle of his thought bubble. I took the book from her and exchanged her finger for mine. When she ran to get a Sharpie, our favourite tool to make her books age appropriate, I picked up my finger to see why exactly Garfield felt he needed to use the F-word.

"Fat." The word I was staring at was "fat."

"This is not the F-word," I said, breaking into hysterics as I showed Adam.

"Yes, it is!" A wide-eyed Lina said, the uncapped Sharpie poised to strike the offending word. "F-A-T; fat," she said, acting like I couldn't read.

It suddenly dawned on me why this was the F-word.

"Yes, baby. You're right. 'Fat' is not a word we use to describe people. Thank you!" She smiled, eliminating it with a single strike from Garfield's vocabulary.

The years after those months of postpartum madness were crazy, but I felt fortunate that they only consisted of the normal "craziness" of motherhood.

EXPLANATORY NOTES ON MY FIRST DESCENT INTO MADNESS

The initial sadness I felt after giving birth may easily have been the "baby blues." According to Lamaze International, the baby blues is a normal adjustment period that 60–80 percent of new mothers experience.[4] It is not a mood disorder, although it includes feelings of sadness, worry, and irritability. Fortunately, it generally dissipates after about two weeks. Generally speaking, only when these mild feelings of sadness and anxiety persist after the initial two weeks should a woman be concerned that she may have a postpartum mood disorder.

It is also worth mentioning here that there is also a condition described as the "baby pinks." Women with the pinks become *elevated* in their moods. They are not simply happy but are unusually euphoric — to the point of not really needing sleep, yet feeling refreshed, and of being overly talkative and unnaturally energized, considering they have only recently given birth. Women experiencing these symptoms should be monitored carefully to ensure they are not manic or hypomanic. This is especially important considering that, in most cases, postpartum psychosis stems from, or is deemed a variant of, bipolar mood disorder.

The disturbing thoughts that I experienced, such as the one involving my baby's fontanel being punctured, are also common symptoms many new mothers experience. These intrusive thoughts are involuntary. In fact, some speculate that up to 90 percent of new parents, both moms and dads, experience these unwanted, often terrifying, thoughts *at least* once. Intrusive thoughts in the postpartum period can take many forms and can be violent, sexual, or religiously blasphemous in nature. Oddly enough, a common postpartum intrusive thought involves poking the baby's fontanel. Other frequent thoughts include the baby drowning or falling out of a window.

Intrusive thoughts can be *what if* in nature. As in, "What if I drop the baby?" or "What if the baby drowns?" They might also manifest as images in one's mind. These mental images are different from visual hallucinations, which are a symptom of psychosis. Visual hallucinations involve seeing things in the outside environment in the absence of external stimuli. Based on my personal experience, unlike intrusive thoughts, visual hallucinations don't feel like they are in your head or are a product of your mind. Visual hallucinations feel real, as though they truly exist outside your body. To my knowledge, the things I saw in my first foray into psychosis were not hallucinations. Those images were confined to my mind, and were therefore intrusive thoughts that presented as mental images.

Intrusive thoughts on their own do not constitute psychosis and are not indicative that one is developing psychosis. Nevertheless, they often cause severe distress to mothers and can cause them to experience postpartum anxiety or depression. If such thoughts become repetitive and cause the person to engage in compulsive behaviours to reduce their frequency, the mother may be experiencing postpartum obsessive-compulsive disorder.

Had my symptoms remained as sadness, anxiety, and unwanted intrusive thoughts, it might have meant I had postpartum depression, postpartum anxiety, or maybe even postpartum obsessive-compulsive disorder. All of these, like postpartum psychosis, are treatable. What I believe made my symptoms cross into the territory of postpartum *psychosis* was the delusional notion I developed that my mother and my husband were capable of acting on the violent thoughts occurring in *my* mind.

Subsequently, I developed ever-worsening delusions. "Delusions" are abnormal beliefs or fixed beliefs that are not grounded in reality. Some of the delusions I experienced included the conviction that my baby was some kind of adult and not really a baby, that my child had autism, that my husband wanted to sexually assault our baby, and that my husband was having an affair.

It was these delusions, and *not* the sadness, anxiety, or initial intrusive thoughts, that indicated that what I was experiencing was more than postpartum depression, anxiety, or obsessive-compulsive disorder.

PART 3

10: ATTENTION GRAB

TWO LINES, NOT ONE. I COULDN'T BELIEVE I WAS finally pregnant again. "Happy anniversary, honey. We're having a baby," I said, hurrying out of the washroom. I wrapped my arms around Adam and cuddled into him.

I had resisted getting pregnant for years, fearful of what I now believed had been postpartum depression. Though I had no official diagnosis from a doctor, my research had me convinced. Friends and acquaintances had moved on to babies two and three, but I held fast, confident that I didn't want to go down that path again.

As Lina grew older and more independent, and as I realized how much I enjoyed being a mother, my resolve started to weaken. I decided I wanted another baby.

We tried, but every pregnancy test confirmed the same thing. That I wasn't pregnant.

As Lina's fifth birthday rapidly approached, it had been a year since I fell prey to baby fever.

"You sure you don't have some secret shares in this company?" Adam had asked one day, waving an empty pregnancy test kit box at me. I was spending a small fortune on my desire for baby #2 and it wasn't paying off. Until the day when it finally did. We danced like two kids on Christmas morning and announced the good news to family and friends.

. . .

I could see from the call display that it was Zara on the telephone.

Zara and I had been friends for longer than I could remember. Best buddies from my earliest memories, we were more opposite than not. She was tall. I was short. She loved dresses and even wore them to parks and sand pits. I hated them and needed a really good excuse to be found in one. Also, she cried a little too much for my liking, especially around bees and wasps.

That changed as we grew older and started sharing more interests. As teens, we became passionate debaters, or maybe it was just that we liked to argue, which often landed us in trouble. One time, we were so heavily embroiled in a dispute that we didn't notice that our train had announced its final stop, let everyone out, and closed its doors before heading back in the direction we'd come from. That day we learned that it's not easy to pry open subway doors.

Since our teenage years, we shared almost everything with each other – including the details of missed periods or episodes of spotting. So if anyone knew to check up on me about anything, it made sense that it would be her. "Are you worried?" Zara asked. She had been in and out of the country for most of my first pregnancy and the year after Lina was born, so me spotting while pregnant was new to her but not me.

"Nah, I'm not too concerned," I replied into the phone. "I had the same issue when I was three months into my pregnancy with Lina, and it turned out to be nothing. I'll give you a shout when I get back," I said, before hanging up.

Adam and I were headed for an ultrasound, just to make sure all was well with the pregnancy. I was convinced nothing was seriously wrong.

I lay on the ultrasound table watching the screen. I was excited to see my baby, even if it was only the size of an apricot or a golf ball. I couldn't really make anything out, and this technician sucked. She wasn't helping by staying silent.

"Excuse me a moment," the technician finally said in a heavy Eastern European accent, suddenly dropping her ultrasound wand. Before I could wonder what was going on, another woman entered the room.

"You say you are about fourteen weeks pregnant?" the new woman asked, picking up the wand and going over my stomach again.

I nodded. Who was this expressionless, middle-aged woman, and why was she here?

"Well, I'm sorry. Whatever is in here looks like it never got past ten weeks, and it has no heartbeat," she said nonchalantly. She cast aside the wand, like whatever was in my stomach wasn't even worth the two seconds she'd spent looking at it.

I got up on my elbows, unable to really process the blow I'd been delivered.

"Do you have someone here with you that you want me to call in?" the technician asked kindly, taking in my stunned face.

"Yeah, my husband, Adam," I responded mechanically. She hurried out of the room, leaving me alone with the robot doctor. The doctor pulled up the scan for Adam and repeated what she'd said to me in the same unfeeling, unsympathetic way. I'd heard that doctors who specialized in radiology tended to be the ones with the fewest people skills, and her behaviour confirmed this theory.

"This baby stopped developing weeks ago. I can't believe you didn't notice a change of symptoms. Your body hasn't registered its demise, but you'll miscarry once it does," she said, in a monotonous tone of voice. She didn't even have the decency to act like the fetus was real; she behaved as if my baby was nothing more than an object I could stop carrying around and get rid of.

"Maybe you can try again for another," the robot doctor said, before motioning to my pile of clothes and walking off.

Adam stayed with me, rubbing my back as tears rolled down my face.

• • •

It had taken a full two weeks from the time I found out the baby had stopped growing to when I actually miscarried. During that interval, I truly felt I'd had enough time to grieve my loss and be at peace about it. It helped too that I had the support of my sister, Mariya, who had moved back from Buffalo the previous year.

"Check out his mullet!" Mariya yelled, hitting pause on an old video of Adam and me so I could take it in. He looked hilarious, and I couldn't believe that's what he'd looked like when we got engaged. Where she'd dug up footage of the surprise party our college friends threw us was a mystery. However she had managed it, it was the perfect pick-me-up to help me get over my grief.

I shrieked with laughter as Mariya kept hitting pause to give voice animatedly to Adam's thoughts. I couldn't help but wonder if it was all that laughter that actually helped my body release my baby later that evening at my parents' house.

I flushed my little baby down the toilet after naming him "Ali" in my head. Disturbing as it felt to watch him swirl into oblivion, Dr. Menko had told me that's what I should do when my body finally decided to let go. Ali was the size of a large peach, but nowhere near as round or robust. I thought I could make out a huge head but couldn't be sure.

"Are you done?" my mom asked gently from outside the bathroom door. There wasn't enough space in her bathroom for us both to fit, but after showing her my loss, she'd let me have a moment to myself so I could do what I needed. I emerged, and she wrapped me in a tight embrace while I wept.

· · ·

About five days later, I woke up feeling strange. I felt like I was in a deep pit, one that I couldn't climb out of. Stranger still was that I seemed to have forgotten how to smile. No matter how hard I tried, I couldn't lift the corners of my mouth. Even when I managed to lift them, they'd immediately droop back down. I was confused.

"Let's go to the mall," Adam announced. We went. At the mall, I kept finding myself staring at all the passers-by as they chatted and smiled effortlessly. I tried my best to mimic their faces and force mine to look like theirs, but no matter how much I struggled, I couldn't make it happen.

I'd always read that frowns took more effort than smiles, so what was happening now was bewildering. What enabled the people around me to be so carefree and happy? It felt like there wasn't an ounce of happiness in the world, in my world at least.

I was so obviously miserable that Adam took the next day off from work to accompany me to Dr. Menko's office. A week after my miscarriage I'd gone from grieving, to being totally fine, to suddenly being unhappy again.

"I'm sad and miserable," I said to Dr. Menko as she sat down at her desk. She cast a glance at my chart in front of her, taking in the illegible notes scrawled on the lined paper. She turned and nodded empathetically.

"You just had a miscarriage, what, like last week?"

I nodded.

"Give yourself a break, it's normal," she said, patting my knee.
"But I feel like I've grieved over that already," I said.
"Cut yourself some slack," she said, getting up. "You'll be fine."

• • •

It is surprising that I sought help from the same doctor who had so nonchalantly dismissed my concerns the first time. This is especially significant because studies reveal that women of colour are less likely to seek help for mental-health concerns. Moreover, racialized women, particularly Black and Latina women, are significantly less likely to seek out help for postpartum mood disorders than white women are.

In my own work with postpartum women and families, 90 percent of the women I assist and support are white, despite the fact that I live in one of the most multicultural countries in the world. It is only in recent years that I have started receiving calls for help from women of colour. Prior to that, I would have to say that 100 percent of the women I was helping were white.

The fact that women of colour are less likely to seek help than their white counterparts has been attributed to many factors, including cultural perceptions about mental health and motherhood, stigma, and healthcare costs (in countries that lack universal healthcare).[1] What doesn't make sense is that even when women of colour do go to the doctor, they are less likely than white women to be screened for postpartum mood disorders.[2] This is deeply alarming, considering that racialized women are nearly at twice the risk for developing one.[3]

• • •

"How come you're still not ready?" Adam asked.

I was slumped in the old office chair, still in my pajamas and staring glassy-eyed at the computer screen. I had been trying to get tips to better organize my house with the time I'd taken off from work.

"I don't feel like going anywhere," I said, not even bothering to look up at him.

"Come on, you promised everyone you would come to Idris's. Idris, Mariya, Mom, Dad, everyone will be expecting you. You have to come. It's the only way you'll get out of the funk you're in," he said, coming to lift me from my seat.

I sat like a rag doll, with no will of my own.

"No, really honey. I can't. I just don't feel like myself," I said. Although Dr. Menko had told me I was still grieving over my loss, I wasn't so sure that was what was wrong. All I knew was that I was feeling down.

"Mommy, I want you to come to the party," Lina said a few moments later, pouting unbearably. Did Adam rat me out? She held my hands, and the look on her face forced me to get out of my pajamas and go.

Idris's new place was beautiful. At any other time, I would have spoken animatedly about how open-concept and well-appointed his home was, how it looked straight out of one of the decorating magazines I loved to pore over. I would have checked out the space and gotten details on everything I loved, like where he bought his lamps or his stunning Saltillo tiles. But nothing seemed of interest to me that day.

Regardless of my party-pooper disposition, everyone was super kind and gentle with me, asking me how I was doing and offering to get me food. I kept feeling like I couldn't get enough air into my lungs and needed to take in multiple short breaths to compensate. I couldn't figure out exactly what the problem was, but I was secretly happy that everyone was assuming I was still grieving over my miscarriage.

All this weird breathing behaviour made me wonder if I was desperate for attention. Could that be it? I wasn't really the type to be so needy, but I couldn't figure out why else I was acting asthmatic when I wasn't. As the evening wound down, I left, still unable to put a finger on what was making me feel so incredibly sad.

11: LOOPY THOUGHTS

ANOTHER PARTY WAS ON THE AGENDA FOR THE NEXT day, this time with Adam's side of the family. I made it clear to him that I was not in any mood to go.

"Last chance," Adam said, helping Lina with her shoes, looking up at me hopefully.

"No thanks. Plus, I've got work to do," I said, listlessly motioning to the computer from where I sat slumped in the swivel chair.

"Okay, if this what you want," he said, giving me a peck on the cheek. Lina threw her arms around me and gave me a big hug and kiss.

"Bye, Mommy," she shouted as the door closed.

I looked at the computer screen and then slowly began swivelling in my chair. Why was I feeling sad? Was I sad about the miscarriage? I didn't think so. I knew I felt peace about it and thought maybe it was for the best. Was it about Adam? I couldn't think of anything out of the ordinary he'd done to irritate or upset me. I felt confused at not being able to pin my feelings of sadness onto any particular thing.

Better get back to organizing, I thought, straightening myself up in front of the computer.

Better get back to organizing.
Better get back to organizing.
Better get back to organizing.

I sat up higher, perfectly still, concentrating on what was unfolding in my mind. Why was my mind repeating this mundane thought like a broken record? I willed my mind to stop the incessant repetition.

Better get back to organizing.

It persisted. I tried harder, even squeezing my eyes shut tightly so I could really focus.

Better get back to organizing.
Better get back to organizing.

I shook my head, feeling like something in there must be stuck. I raced to the washroom, stripped off my clothes and jumped in the shower. A hot shower was my solution to all of life's mundane problems, worries, or pains, and it usually worked. The water whipped intensely at my body. I moved around, letting it soak into every part of me. *Better get back to organizing*, the refrain continued over and over.

I turned up the heat from intense to blistering. My hand shook with fear at the realization that the scalding water had done nothing to stop the repetitive thoughts.

• • •

"Mommy!" Lina came running to me and planted a kiss on my face. She seemed oblivious to the fact that I was lying unresponsive on the couch, my curly hair spread out like Medusa. She ran off to her room.

"What's wrong with you?" Adam asked, alarmed. *He* had obviously noticed.

"I don't know," I whispered. I lay there, lost in the endless loop in my mind.

"Is there something I can do?" he asked.

"No," I whispered, preoccupied by the thought.

"Can I get you something?"

"No."

"I'm gonna put Lina to bed and then I'll be back," he said, going to help Lina.

Why was the thought not leaving? Would it ever stop? How come I couldn't control my mind? This last question made me even more sad than I already was. "Please God, help me," I pleaded silently. I had always been taught to believe in God as the Creator and the One who controlled everything, and so I pleaded with Him to stop whatever was happening to me.

Better get back to organizing.

Adam came and sat down by my legs, rubbing them up and down and giving them an occasional squeeze. I lay there silently, consumed by the repeating thoughts and pleading to God for help. Sad, trapped, and alone, I felt forsaken by God, the one to whom I had been unsuccessfully pleading for the past three hours. I started crying, stricken by the thought of being forsaken by God.

"Wow, it's 2 a.m.," Adam said suddenly. "Do you want me to stay here with you?"

"No," I whispered.

"Do you want to come to bed?"

"No," I whispered.

"Okay then," he said, sounding a bit annoyed. "I'm gonna hit the hay." He bent down, gave me a kiss on the lips and got up to leave.

Better get back to organizing.
Better get back to organizing.
Better get back to organizing.

"Can you sit back down for a minute?" I asked, thinking maybe I should tell him what I was feeling. He sat back down, seemingly eager to listen to what I had to say.

"I feel like God's forsaken me," I said slowly.

Adam leaned forward, looking at me quizzically. "What do you mean?" he asked.

"I've been asking God to help me, help me feel like myself. But He's just not helping me, no matter how much I ask," I said, unable to stop the tears from flowing. I looked over at him, eager to hear what he had to say.

His face narrowed and he looked stern.

"Can you stop with the exaggerating?" he burst out. "So many women have miscarriages. You're not the first one, okay? I'm sick and tired of how long you're dragging this out for, Aaisha. Get over it and move on." He stood up and stalked off.

I sat up stunned. What just happened?

I suddenly felt disembodied, watching myself as a cruel master's puppet, strings and all. The puppet master was making me do whatever he wanted regardless of how I felt. At that moment, I felt like I was privileged with unique insight, insight that no one but I had, about the senselessness of life, particularly mine.

Sleep began pushing down on my eyelids. I got up and walked to bed and climbed in beside Adam, who was already asleep.

. . .

I woke up, feeling a little better. Even though the thoughts were still there, repeating on an endless loop, I felt a little more hopeful, with a sense I could overcome what was plaguing me.

Adam, Lina, and I went to Pizza Hut that evening to celebrate my improvement. We ran into Adam's old friend from high school, Joseph. He looked like he was still in high school, with his varsity jacket and huge smile. Adam introduced us all before chatting.

Better get back to organizing.

"Sorry, I don't want to sound rude or anything, but is everything okay with you?" Joseph's voice suddenly broke into my thoughts. "You look like you're so down or something," his voice trailed off.

I shook my head at his concerned face.

"I'm just tired," I muttered, pink with embarrassment. I turned away, hoping he'd take the hint and leave, or at the very least leave *me* alone. More sadness gripped me at the realization that even complete strangers could tell that there was something wrong with me.

. . .

"Hey, Aaisha! Sorry, did I wake you?" Zara asked the next day. It was late afternoon, but she knew I was a notorious catnapper, capable of snoozing even while standing if the conditions were right.

"Oh, hi," I said tiredly, sitting up in bed as I fumbled with the phone. "No, not at all."

"Just wanted some advice on a problem," she continued. As she spoke, the familiar thought came to join the discussion.

Better get back to organizing.

"Okay, right, okay, yes, okay," I heard myself saying to Zara. It was hard to focus on what she was saying alongside the incessant thought in my head, competing for attention.

"So do you think I'm right to do that?" I heard Zara finally say.

"Yes, it makes sense," I said, trying to sound confident, although I couldn't really remember what we were discussing. I hung up shortly after. I felt like a bad friend. I'd just agreed with something, but I couldn't even remember what her problem was, let alone what she was planning to do about it. I called her back.

"Hey, Zara. Sorry, but please don't listen to anything I said earlier," I said. "Something's wrong with me, and I don't think I'm in a position to be giving advice to anyone right now." My voice began to break as I thought of what was happening.

"What's wrong?" she asked, genuine concern in her voice.

"I just don't feel like myself. My mind won't turn off and keeps repeating the same thoughts over and over again. I'm exhausted, and I just want to go back to being myself." I was rambling and crying now.

"I'm coming over," she said.

"No, don't." Lina was reading in her room. I hadn't been acting like myself for close to a week, and the last thing I wanted was for Lina to hear me bawling to Zara.

I heard knocking at my door less than fifteen minutes later and was surprised to see Zara when I opened it. After letting her in, I ran back to my room and dove under the covers, making sure to pull them over my head. I didn't want her to see what a mess I was. I heard her making some chit-chat with Lina, asking if she wanted a sandwich or cookies or something.

I heard the door to my room closing gently. I could feel Zara sitting down next to me on the bed, her hand on my arm. "Tell me what's wrong, Aaisha," she said. Her request had equal parts kindness and firmness.

"Something is wrong with my mind. I can't seem to control what I'm thinking," I said.

Zara pulled back the covers and offered me some herbal tea. As I sat up to take it, I saw sincere concern in her eyes but also confusion, like what I was saying didn't make sense. I couldn't blame her. The very idea of a thought I couldn't control, repeating itself over and over again, didn't make sense to me either.

"I don't want to think this thought, but it keeps popping up in my head, like an endless chorus or something." I took a sip from the cup, more to show that I appreciated the gesture of her bringing it than out of thirst, and then placed it down dismissively.

She put a slice of apple in my hand. I shook my head. I had no appetite.

"I just want to be me. What's wrong with me?" I moaned.

"Have you told Adam this stuff, about the thoughts?" she asked.

I shook my head again. Anger swelled up in me as I recalled him accusing me of exaggerating what I was going through.

"Have you eaten anything today?" she asked.

Yet again I shook my head.

Her eyes widened. "You shouldn't be by yourself. You're not well. When Adam comes home, I'm going to tell him that you need to stay with your mom while he's at work." I could see that Zara was taking charge, but I disagreed with her assessment of the situation. She persisted, explaining all the reasons it made sense: my mom could help care for Lina, she could prep my food.

"I can't agree more," said a voice. Adam had just walked in and was looking from Zara to me.

I shook my head. I was not going to go. I had stuff to do and didn't have time to laze about my mom's feeling depressed. "I'm not going anywhere," I said.

"Then I'll just have to carry you there," Adam announced, walking over to me.

PART 3

"Please, no. Let me stay here. I have work to do," I said pleadingly, looking over to Zara for help. I saw her standing, arms folded across her chest, looking down at me with sadness but also resolution. I realized then that she was on Adam's side for this one.

"Fine," I said hopelessly, seeing Adam approach. "I'll go!" I yelled, pushing him away.

12: CINNABON TO THE RESCUE

"YOU HAVE TO EAT," MY MOM SAID WHEN I SHOWED UP at her house. She'd been tipped off about my arrival, no doubt by Zara. Squinting as the light inside the house dazzled my eyes, I suddenly realized the near-darkness that mine had been in for the past several days.

"You'll feel better once you eat," she continued, buzzing about with dishes and cutlery. "Look what's here. Your favourite!" A plate of lamb biryani landed in front of my face.

"Uncle Bilal sent it over especially for your dad, but he's decided to let you eat it," my mom said.

I looked over at my dad, who was smiling at me like he'd just contributed something monumental to a war effort and nodded gratefully. My mother watched like a hawk as I took a couple of nibbles. There was just no room anywhere inside of me because the thoughts filled up all available space. I excused myself from the table.

Better get back to organizing.

I went to lie down.

Better get back to organizing.

The thoughts repeated endlessly. They weren't fast, just boring and repetitive, like they were trying to chip away at whatever resolve I had left.

I lay down, exhausted. I couldn't figure out how to get them to stop. The repetition meant that my mind wasn't turning off, which was something I suddenly realized was essential to being able to fall asleep.

• • •

"Zara's here!" my mom yelled up at me the next morning. I trudged down the stairs from the bedroom where I'd spent the night, the one that had been my brother's when we were growing up. It was actually my dad's office now, but it had a bed in it because he loved to power-nap between all the papers he was busy writing. My dad and I often joked that sleeping was a superpower we both shared.

Unfortunately, it felt like I hadn't slept a wink. My mind had refused to shut down thanks to the thoughts. I didn't want to go out with Zara, but I knew I had little choice. It was probably better for me to be out and about rather than sit like a zombie in front of Lina.

I got in the car and sat there silently while Zara drove around doing errands: mailing one thing, picking up another. "My brother wanted me to drop this package off for Idris," she said, pulling up in front of my brother's office building. It was actually a condo, with offices taking up the lower floors.

Nodding as he noticed us in the car, Idris made his way over, looking clean-shaven and smartly dressed. I thought of what I looked like in comparison: a mess. I could see frizzy bits of my hair hanging like limp antennas in front of me and knew my face was wet with tears and maybe even snot.

He took the package from Zara and came around to my side.

I rubbed my nose with the back of my hand. I didn't want him to see what I looked like.

"Hey, can you *please* just be happy?" he said cajolingly, opening the door and lowering his face to my level.

"I want to be happy, but I can't, because my mind won't stop," I burst out. Tears fell furiously while I groped around for tissues.

"Hey, hey," he said, alarm abruptly filling his voice. "Is there anything I can do to help?" he asked, trying to rein in my tears by putting his arm around my shoulder. I shook my head, confident there was nothing anyone could do. How could anyone help me if I couldn't even control the thoughts in my own head?

"Look, whenever I feel overwhelmed or sad, I pray to God for help and He always helps. Promise me you'll pray to God," he said, gently giving me a shake. "Promise me that, okay? I promise that I'll pray for you too," he said. "And if there is anything else I can do for you, like pay for a psychologist or anything, let me know, okay?"

I nodded gratefully. I felt a kiss on top of my head.

• • •

"Dad?" I said, from the living room sofa.

My dad shot up from the armchair across from me. It was a shockingly fast movement for a man in his sixties. He peered at me, ready to grant any request I might have for him.

"Do you have something I can listen to the Quran on?" I asked slowly, thinking of my promise to Idris.

"Yes, I will get you something right now," he said, before bolting up the stairs. Moments later, he was fiddling with a bulky device emblazoned with the word "Walkman." Once a rare status symbol, it was merely a relic from the '80s now. It looked like it belonged in a museum. Equally archaic headphones, similar to the huge earmuffs I'd sported every winter as a child, were attached to it.

"This is beautiful," he said, shoving in an old cassette tape and positioning the headphones over my ears. He hit play.

A sound like singing filled my ears, drowning out the thoughts. The thoughts were floundering, fighting to stay afloat on the melodious waves, surfacing only occasionally. Defeat.

"Is it safe to have it on that loud, sweetie?" my dad would shout at me once in a while, coming over to check on me. Each time I would give him a thumbs up and smile weakly.

The thoughts were fighting back more with each passing day, screaming to be heard. The only way to drown out their wretched cacophony was to turn up the volume.

• • •

Better get back to organizing.

The thought blared loudly in my head. My eyes flew open at the sudden realization that the Quranic recitation I was listening to had stopped. I looked down and saw that I was still cradling the Walkman.

"No more listening for you. You've been blasting this stuff for three days straight. You're going to go deaf," Adam announced, standing over me. My headphones lay dangling from his hands, just out of reach. Anger swept over me as I sat up and tried to get them back, but he kept swinging them as though we were playing a game of catch.

"Please, please give them back," I pleaded. "I need them, you idiot. They bring me peace. Give them back. I hate you," I sobbed, still trying to get a hold of them. I couldn't decide which would work better, begging or getting angry, so I opted for a mixture of both.

"Take a bath, change your clothes, and eat some food, then I'm taking you to the mall," he said. "We'll see how peaceful you'll feel then." People relentlessly teased me about my affinity for the mall, and being my husband, he knew it.

Better get back to organizing.

"Leave me alone!" I growled, flopping back down onto the bed. I closed my eyes, hoping he'd take the hint and leave. There was silence, and I imagined he was leaving with a dejected look on his face. I prayed he'd forget and leave behind the headphones.

Thud.

Something hit my shoulder. My eyes flew open in time to see a pillow come crashing down on my face. Thud, my legs. Thud, my chest. Adam was laughing and stood surrounded by an inordinate number of pillows he'd no doubt fished out from the bedroom closet.

"Stop. Stop. Stop. Please stop!" I screamed, shaking, trying to fend off the pillows whacking me in the head.

"Not. Unless. You. Come. To. The. Mall. With. Me," he said, taking an exaggerated breath between each word.

I shrieked hysterically at the top of my lungs. Mariya and my parents came bolting up the stairs, joining us in the bedroom. They pulled him away, pleading for him to be kind and understanding.

"I'm not going to leave until she agrees to come out. She needs to get out and get active, or she'll never be out of this rut." He laid down his weapons. Knowing how stubborn Adam could be, and realizing I might earn back my headphones with good behaviour, I reluctantly agreed to go to the mall.

The thought repeated all the way to the mall, even as Adam led me by the hand toward our favourite entrance: the Cinnabon entrance.

"One large Cinnabon with extra frosting," he said to the woman behind the counter. He looked over at me, grinning. I stared back stone-faced.

Cinnabon, a panacea for all of life's troubles. If I had to write a commercial for the company, here's how it would go: Bad day at work? Cinnabon to the rescue. Trouble with parenting? Cinnabon to the rescue. I could see Adam watching intently as I ate the Cinnabon, apparently waiting for me to announce that Cinnabon had once again come to the rescue! I finished up and gave him a small smile of appreciation. He looked bewildered.

"I'm gonna get you another one," he said, getting to his feet. I shook my head, but he wasn't having any of it. He marched off in the direction of the Cinnabon shop. The second one came with musical accompaniment in my head, to the tune of:

Better get back to organizing.

We walked out of the mall hand in hand, without the Cinnabon having done a single damn thing to help.

• • •

Better get back to organizing.

My eyes jerked open the next morning. I became aware of the thoughts again.

"I have a surprise for you!" Adam announced, standing over me, holding up my headphones. Why wouldn't he just let me be alone with my Walkman?

"Come on down and I'll show you," he said, dangling the headphones teasingly. Maybe it was because of Lina that he wouldn't let up. Lately, she had taken to standing by my bedside, clutching her blanket and watching me warily. For her, I made my way down the stairs.

Butter chicken and naan, some of my favourite Indian foods, were laid out beside fried bananas and strawberries. Everything that would have been on a wishlist for my dream meal as a child lay before me on the table, courtesy of my mother.

"Surprise!" Adam said, adding a pack of dried dates to the buffet. Ramadan, the holiest month of the Islamic calendar, was rapidly approaching. For Adam and me, it not only denoted thirty days of fasting, but also making deliveries of packaged dates for friends and family to help them welcome the month.

"I already have everything ready to go for the deliveries. Aaisha, you can stay in the car if you want, but I know getting out and doing this will make you feel better. It always does," he said excitedly.

I doubted it would work. In fact, I was positive it wouldn't.

"Can you believe I got these little beauties for only four bucks?" he said, cracking open a box. I tried to act impressed as I chewed on a fried banana. The admission that I didn't want to go with him on the date deliveries could come later. Maybe, just maybe, if I played my cards right, he'd give me back my headphones.

"That's way too much — it should've only cost $1.50 for that," my mom said, frowning.

"Too little, too late. I already bought ten boxes of them," he retorted.

"You're always wasting money. When are you going to learn to use your money wisely?" she countered.

"When you stop acting cheap!" Adam snapped back. He got up and stalked off. I heard the washroom door slam shut just as I saw my mom's already tired face crumple.

"I need some air," I said, getting to my feet. Shoving my feet into my shoes, I opened the door.

Everything was a blur as I ran to the ravine a few blocks away from my parents' house. The grassy embankment greeted me, and I sat down with my knees drawn up against my body. Blades of grass bowed in the gentle breeze. I closed my eyes to better experience it and could hear the water running in the stream below.

"Please God, help me. Please help me be my old self. Please just help me," I prayed. My eyes were firmly shut, my hands clasped in front of my face.

I opened my eyes and watched a reddish-orange leaf twirling in the rippling water. It seemed unable to decide which way to go. Then, suddenly, it made up its mind and sailed away toward its destiny. As I turned to watch its journey, I caught sight of Adam rounding the bend toward the ravine, approaching me.

"Why are you here?" I asked, scowling at him.

"Just came out for a stroll," he said, planting himself a few feet away.

"Like I believe that. Did you think I came to jump?" I asked, motioning to the water and the steep twenty-foot drop. He sat down silently beside me, his elbows resting on his knees.

"It's not like I'm crazy," I scoffed. "Why did you act like that to my mom?"

He looked down and shrugged.

"Can't you see how tired she is of taking care of me and Lina while you're at work? Can't you just cut her some slack?"

He nodded, and I could see remorse on his face. Stretching out in the grass, I watched puffs of cloud glide past serenely.

"You can go if you want. I'm gonna stay here for a bit," I said, closing my eyes. An hour later, we got up and headed back to the house. As we neared the door, Adam opened his jacket and gave me back my headphones.

· · ·

Adam took the next day off to accompany me to the doctor. I had entered week two of whatever I was going through, and on the walk back from the ravine we'd both agreed that it was a good time to touch base with Dr. Menko again.

"I'm still sad and miserable," I said as she sat down across from me.

"You're being too hard on yourself. You just had a miscarriage." I usually liked how she downplayed everything, because I hated alarmist doctors. But this time her words didn't sit well with me.

"But I'm over that. I made peace with it," I said. "This feels different, like my mind is stuck." I wanted her to understand that I wasn't experiencing normal, everyday thoughts, but incessant ones. "See, I keep having this stupid thought about organizing my house. It keeps repeating over and over in my head, like a broken record. And I can't get it to stop."

"Ruminating thoughts," she said, nodding. So my condition had a name. It wasn't some bizarre phenomenon that only I experienced.

"Like I said, you're depressed because you're grieving. Does anything help? Does anything make the thoughts get better?"

"Yes," I said, getting excited at the thought that things might not be so bad after all. "Listening to Quran helps."

"That's really good. Anything else?"

"Yesterday, I went for a walk, and it was the first time in weeks I felt serene. I was also able to notice small things that were beautiful, like the rippling water," I said, recalling it.

"You seem to have a lot of insight into how you are feeling. You'll see, you'll be better in no time."

On the way home, we decided a celebration was in order. Adam and I squeezed past the throngs to a pair of seats at our favourite Afghan restaurant.

"I was so scared she was going to say I was crazy and needed to be locked up," I whispered to Adam below the loud chatter.

"There's always next time," he said, taking in a mouthful of rice. My face crumpled. "I'm kidding," he said, catching sight of me. "I just wish she'd given you some meds." His comments flattened what little joy the appointment had brought me.

. . .

It is troubling that despite making a second effort to get help, I was sent home with little more than a pat on the back and some words of encouragement. In general, it takes considerable strength to push past the idyllic expectations one has of motherhood, the stigma around taking psychiatric medications, and anxiety about getting help. Many of us have been conditioned to feel like our mental health is not as important as our physical health. Most women who seek help worry about the stigma surrounding mental-health problems or are concerned their child will be taken from them if they receive that diagnosis. And so, when a woman does pluck up the courage to seek help, there is nothing more frustrating than to be sent home with no care plan or follow-up. I know through my work that this happens to countless women at the hands of indifferent healthcare professionals and that it happens more often to women of colour.

A study by a Harvard fellow published in *Psychiatric Services* found that racialized women, particularly Black and Latina women, are less likely than their white counterparts to receive follow-up or continued care.[1] This was even when *they themselves* actively ventured to seek out care for what was ailing them in the postpartum period. What this shows is that my experience wasn't an anomaly but indicative of a shockingly pervasive trend in how women of colour with postpartum mood disorders are often treated.

13: ANGEL OF DEATH

"WE'VE BEEN INVITED TO FATIMAH'S THIS WEEKEND," Adam said as we rounded the corner on our walk the following day. Adam's aunt had always hosted dinner for the first Ramadan fast, but ever since she'd passed on, his cousin Fatimah had stepped up to claim the mantle.

"What should I tell her?" he asked, turning to get a look at me. I thought about how loud, funny, and boisterous Adam's family was. They reminded me a lot of my own extended family.

"Sure, let's go," I said, remembering how Dr. Menko said I was doing well. I could picture the joy on Lina's face at seeing me dressed up, instead of lying about in sweats. Maybe Adam's family's boisterous ways could also help distract me from the thoughts.

"Are you sure you're up to this?" Adam asked, concern in his voice, as we sat in the car a few hours later, his hand on my thigh.

Though we were parked right in front of Fatimah's house, I was still taking several shaky, shallow breaths. No matter how many breaths I took, there was still the odd sensation that there just wasn't enough space in my lungs. On the upside, no repeating thoughts. Maybe this was a well-deserved break?

"I feel like it's written all over my face that I'm losing my mind."

"We can go home if you like," he offered, a hand ready to turn on the ignition.

"No, let's go," I said, opening the car door. "It'll make my parents happy, and it'll make me happy, if I'm actually able to do this," I said, taking one more shaky breath. I wanted to make my parents happy. I was sure they didn't know what they had signed up for back when they'd opened the door to me two weeks ago. Adam looped his arm through mine as we walked up to the door and rang the doorbell.

"You look terrible," someone said.

"I've never seen you look so bad," said another. Their frankness was something I'd always appreciated, as it was way more preferable than cattiness behind my back. Their brutal remarks now, however, felt a bit much. Each one felt like a blow to my gut.

"I'm still recovering from the miscarriage," I lied, over and over again. Better than the truth, I figured. Not to mention how effective it was at shutting people up almost instantaneously.

"How's Lina?" Adam's cousin Sophie asked, plunking herself down beside me, a plate of food in hand. Samosas, fruit salad, and spiced chickpeas filled her plate. She tilted it forward, motioning for me to help myself to something. I shook my head. I had passed on getting myself any food.

"She's good. She's with my parents," I said, by way of explaining Lina's absence. I smiled, thinking of Lina. She was no doubt having a blast with all her friends, having gone with my parents to the mosque for *iftar*, the dinner where everyone breaks their fasts together.

"I can't believe how brilliant she is," Sophie said, taking a bite of her samosa. I smiled. Sophie was so sweet, and though only twenty years old, had enough sense to talk about things other than how terrible I looked. "I'm pretty sure she's smarter than me," she said, carefully soaking up what spicy sauce was left with the remaining bit of her samosa.

"You know, one time she was actually talking to me about Shakespeare and Confucius," she continued incredulously. "I was like, 'Confucius? Who's that?'" she continued. "Then she told me that he was an ancient Chinese philosopher. What five-year-old talks like that?" she said, laughing bewilderedly.

Lina's smart, too smart. If she's not properly challenged at school, she'll develop behavioural problems. And if that happens, when she grows up, she'll become a criminal. That's why it's better if she dies. If she dies now she'll go straight to Heaven, because that's where innocent kids go when they die.

Water came sputtering out of my mouth.

"Are you okay?" Sophie asked, thumping me on my back with one hand.

I wasn't. Where did such a bizarre thought come from? I didn't believe Lina would develop behavioural problems. And even if she did, I didn't really believe kids with behavioural problems were destined to become criminals. And I certainly didn't want Lina dead. What was going on in my head?

"You're good, you're fine now," Sophie said, mopping up the water I'd sprayed everywhere with her folded napkin. I nodded in thanks, but I was horrified. Catching Adam's eye, I motioned that I wanted to leave immediately.

• • •

Adam's going to leave you.

Adam's going to leave you.
Adam's going to leave you.

The newest thought burst enthusiastically into my mind, unwilling to restrain itself any longer. I was frightened by how close this was to my true fears. I was indeed worried that Adam might leave me.

I grabbed my coat. "I'm going out," I yelled to my mom.

Her face, which looked ten years older than the one I'd seen when I arrived two weeks ago, peered out at me from the kitchen. "But we just came in," she said, unable to hide the exhaustion.

"I need to get some more fresh air. I won't go far," I promised, by way of an explanation. Walking was proving to be more useful than the Walkman.

Adam's going to leave you.
AAAdam is goooing to leeeave you.
Adam's gooooinnnnng ttooooo lleeeeeeave yooou.

I could hear the thoughts slowing down. I couldn't understand how this was possible, but then again, I didn't really care as long as it worked.

"Sorry about that, Mom," I said, coming in. "I feel so much better when I walk."

She nodded, relieved to have me back.

"Why don't you just use the old treadmill in the basement?" she suggested.

My mom was brilliant. I gave her a peck on the cheek for being a genius.

. . .

128

Adam's gooooinnnnng ttooooo lleeeeeeave yooou.

The soreness in my legs bore testament to the hours I'd spent walking: one hour with my mother, one by myself, and the one I had just spent walking on the treadmill. I knew what I was doing was ridiculous and exhausting, but I was desperate to feel better. Then, a solution hit me.

"Hello, Dr. Pace? It's me, Aaisha. Hope you're well. I need an appointment with you ASAP. Whatever time you have, I'll take it," I said, into his answering machine.

"Does tomorrow at five o'clock work for you?" he asked minutes later, calling back.

"Yes," I nearly shouted into the phone. I was grateful to get an appointment so quickly with Adam's and my old psychologist. He'd been so effective in helping us navigate the prolonged illness and death of Adam's father a few years before.

After I walked another hour on the treadmill, sleep successfully shut down my mind.

"You're going crazy," said a black and white cow, chewing her cud. I stared in amazement at her ability to talk. "First it'll be pots, then kettles. They'll all start talking to you, one by one," she warned ominously.

I woke up sweaty, frightened, and needing to pee — badly. Climbing carefully over Lina's sleeping body, I tiptoed to the bedroom door.

What if you meet the Angel of Death in the hallway?

Springing back from the door at this new thought, I retreated to the bed. I didn't want to go to the bathroom if the Angel of Death was waiting for me in the hallway. Dying would actually be a relief, but Adam and my family would think I'd killed myself. How could they know it was because the Angel of Death had unexpectedly taken my soul?

I drew the blanket over me and decided to ignore the urge to pee.

. . .

Oh, oh, you're turning into Kamran.

I recoiled at the thought of Kamran, Adam's uncle. I had only ever seen him the way he was now: helpless. He paced any room he was in, agitated, often murmuring to himself, trying, but not succeeding, to calm himself down. It was hard to imagine him as anything other than what he was today. But Adam insisted that there had been a time, albeit long ago, when he wasn't like this, when he was even brilliant.

Oh, oh, you're turning into Kamran.

My mind continued to scream at me. Why was it suddenly so loud? Thoughts didn't have volume, did they? And why wasn't walking outside working today? It usually did. I shook my head, trying to physically dislodge the booming thoughts as I hurried back to my mom's.

I ran my fingers on the spines of the books on the living room shelf. There it was. I gently pulled out the Quran. Sitting down, I randomly opened it to a page. It opened onto a chapter I had long ago committed to memory in Arabic. Now, I peeked at the translation of the verses:

> Consider the bright morning hours, and the night
> when it grows still and dark. Thy Sustainer has
> not forsaken thee, nor does He scorn thee: for,

indeed, the life to come will be better for thee than this earlier part [of thy life]! And, indeed, in time will thy Sustainer grant thee [what thy heart desires], and thou shalt be well-pleased.

Tears fell as I read, soaking into the tissue-thin pages. I closed the book, kissing its ornate cover before returning it to its place on the shelf.

• • •

As we sat in Dr. Pace's waiting room, I kept murmuring the verses I'd read to myself. They made me feel good inside, even if they didn't do much to stop the thoughts.

Dr. Pace, a tall, thin, bespectacled man, came out and invited us into his office.

"So, tell me, how can I help you?" he said, looking over his thick-rimmed glasses with a comforting smile.

"Yes," I shifted uncomfortably. "I had a miscarriage about three weeks ago and then started feeling down," I said, by way of an introduction. "I am sad and miserable without knowing why, totally exhausted and tired."

He was scribbling fast, trying to get everything down.

"But worse are these repetitive thoughts that I can't turn off. They were about stupid things initially, but now they're downright upsetting and make me feel like I'm going crazy."

"Possibly intrusive thoughts," he said.

"Intrusive thoughts?"

"Yes, thoughts you don't want and find upsetting invading your consciousness. Likely caused by your falling pregnancy hormones." It was nice of him to give a detailed picture of the problem, but I just wanted a solution.

"Does she need medication?" Adam asked, with more than a hint of interest. What was up with him and his desire to plug me up with meds?

"I don't think *that's* necessary," he said.

I got the sense that he frowned on meds, deeming them an unnecessary evil. This sort of matched my own views on the subject. Although I wasn't entirely averse to psychiatric medications, I had a feeling that only people who weren't strong enough to manage what was happening to them needed them.

"But what can I do, Dr. Pace?" I asked, eager for a Band-Aid solution to my problems.

"Do things to get your body to release endorphins or provoke your senses," he advised. "Exercise, take a shower, brush your teeth, drink soothing teas, or try aromatherapy."

Though I had a bit of a bounce in my step as we left his office, I couldn't help but wonder if he'd mentioned brushing and bathing on purpose. Was it that obvious that I had no time or interest in either?

• • •

"I think I'm getting better!" I shouted out to Adam a short while later. Eager to try out Dr. Pace's new tools, I was sitting in the bathtub, drinking a soothing cup of herbal tea. My toothbrush lay nearby just in case.

"Good!" he yelled back. How come he didn't sound convinced?

"We'll sleep in the basement together so you can use the treadmill," my mom said later that evening. Tucked under one arm were two pillows, and a large blanket was trailing from under the other. She looked like a tired child, ready for yet another exhausting sleepover.

I nodded, grateful for her offer.

1:00 a.m.

You're turning into Kamran. Adam's going to leave you.

The combination-compound thought was new, like it was trying to add a bit of spice into my usual roster.

You're turning into Kamran. Adam's going to leave you.

I needed to change the channel on my thoughts, like Dr. Pace had told me. I brushed my teeth and splashed my face with water, dripping some on my head for good measure before going to lie down again.

You're turning into Kamran. Adam's going to leave you.

Wedged between Lina and my mother, I could hear Lina quietly breathing in and out. Even in the dim light, I could tell my mom was staring at me, wide-eyed. I knew if there was more light, I would see sadness on her face as well. I imagined her bottom lip was trembling, as it so often did whenever she looked at me lately. I closed my eyes, if for no other reason than to encourage my mom to close hers.

A checkerboard popped up, twisting, warping, dancing in a frenzy. Then came a spangle of stars, moving to their own beat. Lights: blue, green, fuchsia, and yellow illuminated the checkerboard like I was watching a disco scene unfolding. Cubes: small, big, medium, and ultra-tiny, jumping over each other as they tried to join the fun — all competing for an equal share of attention. I watched the spectacle with a mix of wonder and horror, hoping it would disappear into the darkness just as suddenly as it had mysteriously arrived.

It was no use. I realized it was either the thoughts or the chaotic dance sequence that I would have to contend with, so I heaved my exhausted body onto the treadmill.

3:30 a.m.

Yooooo're tuuuurnnningggg iiiinto
Kaaaammmmmmmrrrrraaaaan.

Then, suddenly, silence. Peace descended on me. I hobbled off the treadmill mesmerized by the sound of silence in my brain. It sounded beautiful, breath-taking. I couldn't believe I'd taken silence for granted for nearly three decades. I closed my eyes, fearing the checkerboard and cubes: nothing.

"Thank you, God, for the silence," I whispered.

14: KICK THE BASTARD

YOU ARE GOING CRAZY.

My mind screamed to the tune of childish playground taunts. Bolting up the stairs, I slammed the door on my way out of my mother's house. It was 11 a.m., and I hadn't slept a wink since I realized silence, true silence, had a sound: nothingness.

Dr. Pace had been right about how endorphins could kick the recurring thoughts to the curb, but he'd forgotten one itty-bitty essential truth. That they would leave me energized. Too energized to fall asleep, even though I was exhausted. So I had to lie there in beautiful silence contemplating the truth of Simon and Garfunkel's song "The Sound of Silence."

You are going crazy.

Relentlessly, mercilessly, they screamed at me now. Thoughts apparently did have volume.

You are going crazy.

They wanted to hurt me so badly that the walking, jogging, and even running were proving to be of little use. They were winning control, overwhelming my mind. I gripped my head, unable to accept the reality of what was happening.

"They're winning, they're winning," I screamed as I tumbled back into my mom's house. I ran to the basement and mounted the treadmill yet again. The cordless phone was still in the treadmill's cup holder, from back when I'd called Dr. Pace. I needed to tell someone what was happening; how the thoughts were winning their battle to gain control over me. I dialed Adam.

"They're winning," I screamed into the phone. I didn't have time to explain before I saw my mom enter the room. I quickly hung up, but not before I heard Adam yell something back at me. What was he saying? I couldn't be sure.

My mom stood eyeing me suspiciously. I tried to act chill, like I was simply walking and nothing had changed significantly. But it had. The thoughts were sounding more like a voice, and worse, they were gaining control over my mind. My mom, however, could not know this. It would kill her to know that no matter what she or I or any of us did, things were going from bad to worse.

"Zara's here," she said quietly.

Anger pulsed through me. I knew there was no way Zara had just shown up randomly. My mother must have called her, probably when I'd bolted out of the basement earlier.

"We need to talk," Zara said, striding over to me with her long legs.

"Fine," I said. "But I'm gonna stay on the treadmill."

Everything that I'd experienced since we last spoke tumbled out of my mouth.

"I think you need to see a doctor again. Five hours of walking? This can't possibly be what Dr. Pace meant. You're small enough as it is. You're going to disappear at this rate," Zara said. I looked down at the clothes that had fit me so well only a few weeks earlier. They hung on me as though I were a hanger. Even my pants bunched over my shoes.

"I already went. Twice, remember? I don't need a doctor. It's like there's two sides to my brain. One side where the intrusive thoughts are coming from and the other side that has me — the real me — in it. I just need people to help me, give voice to the old me. Remind me I'm not going nuts, even force me onto the treadmill."

Zara nodded sympathetically. She was so good at listening. "I still think you should go back to the doctor. Things have changed with you. See what they have to say now."

She was sounding like Adam. Were they in cahoots with each other? Adam was making no bones about the fact that he thought I needed medication. It was almost like he wasn't listening at all to what Dr. Menko and Dr. Pace had said. They clearly felt like I could handle what was happening on my own. I wasn't like *those* people, the type that needed meds because they had no willpower to manage it themselves.

"I can do this on my own," I said, climbing the stairs to the kitchen.

"I'm here," Adam said, stepping into the house.

"What are you doing home so early?" I asked.

"Let's see, my wife calls me screaming about someone winning and then suddenly hangs up. Call me crazy, but that could be why," he said, throwing up his hands. "Now hurry up, I'm taking you to the doctor."

"No!" I shouted, anger mounting at how he was acting, like he was the boss of me. "I don't need to go — I'm better now. Can't you see?"

"You're going to the doctor," he said sternly.

"I just needed some endorphins. It's a miracle!" I shouted.

"You're going to the doctor," he said, his voice like ice.

"No, I'm not."

"Yes, you are."

"I'm *not*," I said, looking to Zara and my mom for some support. I wanted them to tell him I was fine — to confirm how much better I was now. Catching my eye, Zara looked away uncomfortably. I couldn't believe it.

I folded my arms over my chest, eyeing them all. Somber, grave faces stared back at me. After everything I'd been through the past few days, it was now, when I was finally feeling a little better, that they were so concerned? I could feel the corners of my mouth curling upward and couldn't contain the laughter bubbling inside of me. It spilled out suddenly and unexpectedly. I doubled over laughing, holding the stitch in my left side.

Their concerned expressions left, only to be replaced with mortification. "From your faces, it looks like you all think I'm crazy. But it's really you guys who are the crazies," I said, unable to control myself again and breaking into another fit of laughter. My mom's face dropped back to sadness. Adam was laughing too, while Zara had an awkward look on her face.

"See? You know you're acting crazy! That's why you are laughing with me," I said, finally feeling like I was on the same page as everyone else.

"I am *not* laughing with you," Adam said dryly. I couldn't help but wonder what he meant.

• • •

"Hello, I am Dr. Johnson," said the young woman, smiling. She stepped aside so we could come into the examination room. It was one of the smaller rooms, but I didn't care.

It was way past Dr. Menko's consulting hours, so I knew I wouldn't be seeing her, but this new doctor was not at all what I expected. I decided "lithe" was the perfect word to describe her.

"So what can I help you with?" she asked. She tossed her long brown hair as she said this. For a moment I forgot I was at the doctor's, feeling like I was watching a Pantene commercial instead.

"I had a miscarriage three weeks ago, and I think I'm having some type of depression, because I've been sad and exhausted," I said. I remembered Dr. Menko had used the word in conjunction with her assessment that I was grieving. I didn't want this new doctor to latch on to the idea that I was just grieving and dismiss me again. Depression sounded medical, whereas grieving sounded more like an interpersonal problem.

"You've been here twice before in the past two weeks? Less than two weeks?" she said, scanning the notes in my file and looking up. I nodded. "Anything else you are experiencing?" she asked.

"Yes, I also keep having these repetitive thoughts that don't let me sleep and make me think I am going crazy." I took a deep breath before the final bit, the reason I had finally agreed to come to the doctor. "I'm trying to cope, but I feel I'm not getting support," I said, looking directly at Adam. There, I had stuck it to him. Her pen scribbled away at her notepad; this last statement was no doubt being recorded in her notes.

"Is it normal to feel overwhelmed and frightened by your thoughts and to constantly think you're going crazy?" I asked. I knew my question sounded weird, but I didn't care. What I was experiencing was downright disturbing.

"Well, it's definitely not normal, and to be honest, it sounds quite sad," she said. I sensed empathy in her voice. "But let me ask you, do you feel like harming yourself or others? Do you hear voices or see things other people can't?"

I shook my head. I wasn't a violent person. But then again, how could she know that? She wasn't my regular doctor.

"Wait," I said, backtracking. "These voices you're asking about. What would I hear them with, my ears?"

She looked perplexed, like it was a question she'd never before had reason to contemplate. "Yes," she said tentatively. "That's usually how you hear voices, with your ears. So yes, you would hear them with your ears."

My shoulders relaxed, relieved from some of the weight that was on them. So they weren't really *voices* that I was hearing. But I was still confused. What, then, was going on in my head, with the thoughts getting louder?

"But the thoughts in my head are very loud. They sound like voices — but I don't hear them with my ears. I know that they're in my head. Is that kind of voice okay?"

"Is the voice in your head your own, or someone else's?"

"It's mine," I said confidently. Even though I knew it was my voice I was hearing, I also knew that the words it was saying were not my own. I shuddered at the memory of my mind telling me that Lina needed to die.

"But it's telling me really disturbing things, things that are really upsetting me and making me scared." Sadness welled up inside me.

"Well, it really does look like you have depression," she said.

Relief washed over me. I had been brutally honest about everything I was experiencing, and here was my reward: a firm diagnosis.

"It seems like you're handling yourself pretty well and have a lot of insight into your thoughts and feelings. But you know, there are tools like antidepressants that you can take to help you along."

At that, Adam straightened up, looking for the first time like he was keen on hearing what she had to say.

"Do *you* think I need them?" I asked.

"That's up to you to decide; antidepressants are there as a tool for you," said Dr. Johnson.

I thought I saw Adam's shoulders fall.

"If you think I'm doing fine, I'd prefer not to take any medication," I said.

"I'm going to make you a referral to a psychiatrist, just in case things don't get better for you. You won't be seen anytime soon, but that way, if you aren't better, you'll already be in line," she said, tossing her hair a final time before scribbling on her pad.

. . .

For the longest time after recovering from my illness, this appointment with Dr. Johnson really bothered me. Short of diagnosing myself, I couldn't imagine what more I could have said to get a proper diagnosis. I'd accurately described that I felt like I was hearing a voice in my head and yet, after asking a series of strange questions, she added nothing to my understanding of what I was experiencing.

The experience of being undiagnosed happens too often to all women with postpartum mood disorders. However, research reveals that it statistically happens even more often to women of colour. In fact, racialized women with postpartum depression are more likely to have the experience of being undiagnosed than white women, even after going to healthcare providers multiple times.[1] This is concerning when it comes to any postpartum mood disorder, but particularly when it comes to a dangerous condition like postpartum psychosis.

. . .

I went to bed that evening after Adam left, feeling the weight of my eyelids pressing down. No strange objects pranced about, even if my mind was refusing to switch off. "Please God, just let me sleep. Please God, just let me sleep." I mouthed the words to myself.

My parents were at the mosque for *Taraweeh*, the special nightly prayers performed during the month of Ramadan. Under any other circumstance, I would have been right there with them. In fact, I hadn't missed a single year of attending the prayers since I was a little girl. Still, I knew God would understand my missing out this year.

Fearful of what might choose to appear next on the canvas of my mind, I thought of something peaceful, comforting to me. The *Kabah*, a cubic structure in Mecca that Muslims circle, honouring Abraham's shrine to God, came zooming into focus. I could even see the gold embroidery along the top, looping to form the Arabic letters adorning the black cloth. It was majestic.

I was seasoned at conjuring this image in my head. It was a technique I'd perfected back when I was a kid, when my pediatrician had instructed me to focus on good thoughts to quell my childhood anxiety over blood tests.

I envisaged myself inching closer and closer to the *Kabah*, just on the brink of touching it. Maybe I could even kiss it, as people did in pilgrimage. Then out of nowhere I saw it. A man, long dead, hanging from the *Kabah* I had so painstakingly conjured. I took in all of him.

> *Gnarly bony fingers.*
> *Contorted, bluish-gray face angled sharply to the side.*
> *A thickly woven rope cutting into meager neck flesh, drawing open a mouth.*
> *Half-open eyes staring out at me.*

My eyes flew open and I bolted upright, terrified. What was going on? Where did such an image come from? Did I conjure it myself? And if so, why?

Thumping down the stairs two at a time to get to the treadmill, I ran smack into my parents' startled faces. What were they doing home so early from *Taraweeh*? Their mugs of tea hung suspended in mid-air, waiting for an explanation.

"I just don't feel like sleeping," I said, trying to conceal the horror on my face. Changing track, I said, "I think I'll just stay up." I lay on the couch, whispering prayers to myself as my parents drank their tea.

"Please. Please, can you ask God to take me away from this world?" I said suddenly. Alarm clearly registered on their faces. "Please, I am in so much physical pain," I said. It was my first time acknowledging that every nerve and fibre in my body felt like it was on fire. "But the mental agony is worse."

They shook their heads.

I was upset at their clear selfishness. "If you loved me, you would pray for my death. I can't take it any longer."

"We're not praying for that! We are praying for you to get better," my dad said, my mom full-out sobbing beside him. I turned over. I was causing them so much pain; another reason I should be dead.

· · ·

"I only slept from six to eight before those crazy thoughts came back," I said to Adam the next morning, half crying into the phone. "I've only had two hours of sleep in the past three days." My mom's cordless phone was on speaker mode, as there was no way I could hold it myself. My hands were a necessity for the task of supporting myself as I forced my legs to speed-walk on the treadmill.

"Remind me again why you're refusing to take any medication?" Adam asked. I imagined him pulling at his hair.

"Because I can do this!" I screamed, before hanging up on him. Why was he being so dense? If he would just counter the voice in my head and remind me over and over again that I wasn't going crazy, I could overcome this problem by myself.

Like every other evening, Adam came to my mom's house to join us at dinner, but this time he wore a steely look. I was grateful Lina was at Idris's place. I held my plate up for my mom to fill with curried shrimp, another favourite of mine. It didn't taste like my favourite today, but I acted like I was enjoying it so as to make her happy.

"So, Dr. Johnson said she thought I was handling my symptoms well," I said, chewing slowly.

Adam grimaced. "She also said medications could help," he interjected.

"Yes, but she said she didn't think I needed them," I said, scowling. I wanted to be in charge of the narrative. After all, this was about me. "Hey, I forgot to pray," I said, suddenly getting to my feet. We had daily prayers at designated times, and I'd almost missed the sunset one. *Shame*, I thought, heading to my old bedroom. As I began reciting my prayers, I was accosted by what appeared before me.

Tiny socked feet dangling.
Arms hanging limply on either side.
A thick braided rope secured neatly beneath a chin.
Lina's chin.

Then,

You are crazy. Stay away from Lina!

The hair on my arms stood up and sirens blared in my head, sending me into a panic. A blood-curdling scream let itself out of my mouth, just before I broke away from my prayers, flying down the stairs to the basement.

"What the hell?" I heard Adam say.

My heart pounding in my ears, I opened the Quran and flipped to where I'd marked off the verses of comfort and began reciting to myself. The thin pages seemed to be melting away as they soaked up my tears.

I couldn't understand what I'd just seen. I knew it was Lina, but Lina wasn't home. This was different from all the other things I'd experienced, because it didn't feel like it was confined to inside my head. This image had felt real, like it was outside of my body. But at the same time, I knew it couldn't be real, because Lina was with Idris. My hands trembled as I remembered the shrieking thought that had accompanied the image — the one implying that I was a threat to Lina. Snot dribbled from my nose onto the pages, and I tried wiping them off without ruining them.

"What on earth is going on?" Adam had followed me down and now stood across from me, arms crossed, face red and pinched.

How could I tell him what I'd just seen? He'd think I subconsciously wanted to hurt Lina.

"I just need to read this," I sobbed. "God has not forsaken thee, nor does He scorn thee." My tears continued to drip all over the pages as I read the words out loud. "I feel like God's consoling me through this," I explained, through stuttered gasps. "I need to be reminded that I'm not being forsaken or punished …"

"You are not Jesus Christ!" Adam's words hit like a fist to my face. "You are not some special person who God would be consoling through His book!" He was screaming. Before I could even digest what was transpiring, I heard the door slam and him stomping up the stairs.

New sadness gripped me. I looked down at the preamble:

> [This chapter] concerns — and is meant to con-
> sole — every faithful man and woman suffering
> from the sorrows and bitter hardships …

I was not delusional to find the verses comforting.

I was falling from a monumental height, swirling into a dark abyss. I needed someone to remind me that I wasn't losing my mind. Zara. I grabbed the phone.

"You are insane! Insane!" Adam screamed, coming back into the room.

I covered my ears to block out his harsh words, words echoing what the thoughts were saying, but I could still hear him.

"You are selfish. Killing your parents and seriously disturbing Lina with your stubbornness and unwillingness to take any drugs. You are totally insane, do you hear me?" he yelled into my face.

What was wrong with him? Why did he want to make me insane? Punching and kicking, I tried to get past him as he blocked the door with his body.

Finally I shoved him aside. "Get out of my life, you bastard. I want a divorce!" I screamed into his contorted face before racing up the steps. "Kick the bastard out of your house. I'm getting a divorce!" I yelled at my stunned parents before running to my bedroom. Rapid, shallow breathing consumed me as I lay down.

An hour later I crept down the stairs. "Mom? Is he still there?" I asked. I could hear only my parents talking but needed to make sure.

"He left about forty-five minutes ago," my mom said.

Breathing a sigh of relief, I joined my parents. Disturbing their nightly tea ritual was turning into a regular habit of mine.

"Adam's just crazy," I announced. "All he ever talks about is getting me hooked on antidepressants. I think me being like this is really getting to him, and he can't handle it."

"Listen, honey, you can stay here for as long as you want, okay? Just focus on getting better. Don't worry about the way he's been acting or anything else," my dad said kindly. My mom nodded her head. I kissed them both and headed up the stairs again to lie down.

15: TAKE TWO ADVILS

"MAMA, I MISSED YOU SOOOOO MUCH!" I TURNED TO see Lina running toward me, arms outstretched, lips puckered.

"I missed you too, pumpkin," I said, sitting up and smothering her with kisses. Lina's fingers inched around me and found her ratty blanket. Pink and covered with white lambs, it was as old as she was.

She rubbed it under her chin thoughtfully. "How come we never play anymore, Mama?" she asked.

"We will," I said, drawing her into an embrace. Her face tilted toward me for a closer snuggle, revealing her neck. I couldn't help but recall the vision I had seen earlier and the warning that had accompanied it.

A thick braided rope secured neatly beneath a chin.
Lina's chin.
You are crazy. Stay away from Lina!

My heart skipped a beat as horror rose up inside me. "Come downstairs — I think Grandma wants you," I said, rushing her from the room and down the stairs.

Why was the image there? I loved Lina more than anything in the world. I would keep her safe — even from me. Leaving her with my mom, I ran back up.

Dr. Johnson confirmed I was sick with depression, so I knew that much for sure. But could depression make you think vile, evil thoughts? I decided the internet might be able to tell me.

> Depression. Bipolar Depression. Seasonal Depression. Postpartum Depression.

None of them mentioned anything about vile thoughts.

> Postpartum Depression.

Maybe it could happen even with a miscarriage? I decided it couldn't hurt to read about it.

> Postpartum blues — a normal experience — mood lability, tearfulness. No specific treatment is required.
>
> Postpartum depression — depressed or sad mood, tearfulness, loss of interest in usual activities, sleep disturbance.

This was me. It was describing me but was missing a few of my symptoms. Perversely, excitement welled up inside of me as my fingers began dialing Adam.

"Hi, Adam. Sorry about earlier," I mumbled.

"Yeah, okay," he said, clearly not sounding okay.

"I was just thinking maybe you're right, maybe I should get some naturopathic antidepressant or something."

"Fine. Is that all?" he asked.

"Yes, bye. I love you."

He hung up. I went back to reading.

> Postpartum obsessive-compulsive disorder has
> also been reported, where women have disturbing
> and intrusive thoughts of harming their infant.

I bit my lip as I reread the sentence, taking in the words. I thought about the image of Lina and the screaming thought telling me, no, *warning* me that I was a danger to her. Air in my lungs felt like a scarce commodity and I felt light-headed. Feeling the need to do something, I hit redial.

"Adam?" I said, "I want to go to the doctor tomorrow to get some real antidepressants." I thought he would jump for joy, maybe ask me how I was finally coming around.

"Fine," he said, before hanging up. My heart felt heavy. He was still upset. I decided to close the tabs and head down to Lina.

"She fell asleep while you were on the phone," my mom said, nodding her head at the sofa.

I saw Lina draped with my mom's shawl, her body rising and falling rhythmically with each breath. A peaceful contrast to the roiling thoughts in my mind. I sat down and lay my head on her to take in her breathing and her beating heart.

"I'm going to the doctor tomorrow to ask for some antidepressants."

My parents' eyebrows rose dramatically.

"I think I need them. I haven't been able to spend time with or care for Lina, and I think it's about time I got back to being me."

They sat silently until my mom excused herself to go to the bathroom.

"Can I tell you something, Dad?" I asked. I had put my mom through enough hell and didn't want to dump anymore on her.

"Anything," he said. "What is it?"

"Don't tell Mom, 'cause she'll just start to worry, but it's just that some weird things have been happening to me."

He nodded. Encouraged, I continued.

"It's reminding me a lot of what happened to me after Lina was born."

He nodded slowly, ready to accept anything I wanted to share about that dark time in my life.

"See, yesterday, when I was trying to think of good things like the *Kabah*, I saw an image of a dead man hanging from it."

My dad's eyes grew wide.

"It reminded me of when Lina was born. I used to have this image in my head of Lina's fontanel" — I indicated the top of my head, wanting to be as clear as possible — "being smashed with a long iron ..."

"What?" he said, suddenly on his feet. Revulsion replaced the concern and acceptance of seconds earlier. "What are you saying?" he said, voice rising.

I stared at him, unable to respond, paralyzed.

"How could you say such a thing about your baby? How could you? Adam's right, you are crazy."

He was shaking, and I feared he was restraining a strong urge to strike me. I covered my face with my hands to avoid seeing the revulsion on his face. I felt evil, like a monster.

"What's wrong?" my mom asked, emerging from the bathroom. My dad was pacing anxiously.

"I think I need to go to the hospital," I said, my voice breaking at the realization of how truly sick in the head I was.

"I'll tell you what's wrong. Adam's right, she's crazy." My dad turned and stomped up the steps.

"My chest is hurting," I heard him say. My mom followed in hot pursuit.

• • •

"Adam?" I said, calling him again. "I want to go to the hospital right now, I'm scared."

"Tomorrow," he said, in a steely tone.

"I need to go now. I keep having these scary images of dead people hanging." My heart felt like it was in my throat, choking me. I contemplated whether or not I should reveal what I'd seen involving Lina. I decided against it, fearing he'd think I was a monster, too.

"Tomorrow."

"But what am I supposed to do now?" I said, breaking down at the thought of being left to manage the images on my own.

"Take two Advils and go to bed," he said, hanging up.

I lay down in the basement again, wedged between Lina and my mom. Shaky breaths escaped me as I closed my eyes, wondering if my mind would permit me to sleep. A kaleidoscope of colourful images appeared, spinning, swirling, shrinking, and enlarging. I felt myself mechanically zooming in on the image. Decapitated heads, arms, and legs were set a-swirl. They weren't shapes; they were human body parts, outlined in vibrant colours and dancing serenely. My eyes flung themselves open at this horrifying realization. I moved away from Lina. I was sick, really sick, and I couldn't trust myself to be anywhere near her.

"I don't want Adam to be my power of attorney if I lose my mind," I said, dictating a living will to my mom. *Take two Advils and go to bed.* I kept hearing his words from earlier, further cementing my sadness. I could feel my mother's embrace tighten and hear her sniffling. I knew she would have driven me to the hospital if she'd known how to drive.

"I need to go to the bathroom and eat before the fast starts," my mom said uncomfortably, loosening her hold on me.

I dragged myself upstairs, not wanting to be left alone in bed with Lina. I didn't trust myself.

· · ·

Dzst, dzst, dzst.

Buzzing shocks zapped my brain, sending shivers through me. I grabbed my head, trying to make sense of what was going on. Just then, I felt the pull of an overwhelmingly powerful magnetic force tugging my head to one side. I felt myself lurch in the direction of the pull. I couldn't stop even if I wanted to.

I slid across my mom's laminate kitchen floor, both mesmerized and horrified by what was happening to me. The Quran. It was the sound of the Quran emanating from my parents' CD player that was responsible for the magnetic pull.

I gasped at the realization, even as I continued to be pulled unwillingly. God was pulling me toward Him, just as the Devil was trying to establish himself in my head. It was a battle of apocalyptic proportions, and my mind was the battlefield. At that very moment, I saw that this explained all I'd been experiencing over the past several weeks: it was the Devil who had been telling me Adam was going to leave me, that I was going crazy, and to stay away from Lina.

No, that didn't make sense; the Devil wouldn't want me to stay away from Lina. That bit must have been from God. Having finally reached my destination by the CD player, I shut it off. I finally knew what all the weeks of build-up were about, and I needed to stage an intervention.

"I need help!" I told my dad. He'd just returned to the living room from wherever he had been during my moment of divine epiphany.

"I need to find a Muslim doctor!" I screamed into his confused face.

"What? Why?" he asked, looking from my mom to me.

"I'm really sick, so I need a doctor," I said urgently.

"But why a Muslim doctor?" he asked. God, why was this man, who was usually so intelligent, being so dense?

"Because only a Muslim doctor will understand," I said, rolling my eyes with frustration. On top of being sick, which I knew I was, I now knew that my mind was also the site of a divine battle between God and the Devil. So, I needed a Muslim doctor who I could explain everything to. A Muslim doctor could treat the symptoms of my illness while allowing God and the Devil to wage their battle uninterrupted.

I knew from an abnormal psychology class I'd taken in university that there was a high chance any other doctor might interpret my religious insights as a delusion. But I knew *I* was not delusional, so I needed a Muslim doctor who would be able to understand what I was going through while providing me with the drugs I needed to cope.

"Explain why you don't want to go to the hospital anymore, but now need to find a Muslim doctor?" my dad asked.

"I need a Muslim doctor because only a Muslim will understand what God and the Devil are doing to me. Other doctors will think I'm crazy," I said.

"To me, it sounds like you *are* crazy," he said with frustration.

I lay down on the sofa, feeling dejected. I would call Zara. She would help.

"Hello, Zara? Sorry to bother you so early, but I wanted to know if you knew any Muslim doctors?" I asked.

"What's going on? Why?"

Fearing she wouldn't understand, I decided not to tell her. "I want to start on some antidepressants but with a Muslim doctor."

"Aaisha, any doctor can help you with that."

"Okay," I said. I made a mental note to leave out any religious stuff lest the doctor think I was delusional. "Adam's mad at me, so can you take me?" I asked. I wasn't sure how she'd react, what with it being seven in the morning and a workday.

"Be ready for eight," she said, before hanging up.

"Where are you going now?" my dad asked, from where he was still watching me like I was a strange specimen.

"Zara's going to take me to the clinic at eight," I said, running up the stairs to get ready.

. . .

Though I never experienced religious delusions during my first experience with postpartum psychosis, for some reason they emerged in my second. Despite what people might think, they had nothing to do with my race, culture, or religious background as a Muslim. Postpartum psychosis is not a case of religious fervor gone amok. Nonetheless, religious undertones to delusions are recognized as a common feature of postpartum psychosis.

Andrea Yates,[1] Dena Schlosser[2] and Deanna Laney[3] all experienced severe religious delusions prior to taking the lives of their children. One believed she was possessed by the devil, another felt she needed to give her youngest child to God, and the last was operating under the delusion that God was telling her to sacrifice her children as a test of her faith. Such delusions have even been reported by women who identify as staunch atheists. For example, in her memoir on postpartum psychosis, entitled *Inferno*,[4] Catherine Cho writes about the vivid religious delusions she experienced, despite not being particularly religious.

No one really knows why religious delusions play a recurring role in cases of postpartum psychosis. From personal experience,

I have my own theory. I think it has to do with the fact that the symptoms one experiences with this illness come on so suddenly, connect to your own personal fears, and are so bizarre, that there is no way to make sense of them except by attributing them to supernatural or spiritual forces.

. . .

Dzst, dzst, dzst.

Despite the Quran recording being off, the divine battle raged on. I wasn't sure now if my mind was merely the battlefield or if forces were fighting for control of my mind. Either way, it was wreaking havoc on me, causing me to shake uncontrollably and twitch.

"What *happened* to you?" Zara asked, unable to hide her shock when I opened the door for her. I shrugged, feeling a twitch under my eye.

"Look, Adam is coming with us, so before he gets here, I want to tell you something," she said, leading me to the sofa. "I've been researching some stuff, and it says it's really important to tell the doctor everything that's happening to you, okay? Don't be scared. It's the only way they'll know what type of medication is right for you."

I could feel the sadness and anxiety rising up within me, lodging in my throat. "But I'm afraid to tell them some stuff, like that my mind keeps telling me I shouldn't be near Lina." Tears splashed on my hands as I imagined people coming and removing a kicking, screaming Lina from me, whispering that I was a bad mom, even dangerous.

"I would never harm Lina, but my mind keeps acting like I'm going to do something to her. That's why I want medication. I want that to stop," I said.

A car beeped outside. Adam had just pulled up in the driveway.

I got to my feet. "Tell them that. Tell the doctor what you just told me," Zara said, giving my hand a squeeze.

16: JUMP

"I CAN'T BELIEVE HOW FAST WE MADE IT HERE," ADAM announced as he pulled over.

"I'll park while you get her registered," Zara said.

Taking my hand in his, Adam led me to the familiar clinic. He was back to being gentle and kind. This early in the morning, the clinic was completely empty. My feet echoed on the white laminate tiles as we emerged from the elevator. I popped my head into the reception area to let them know I was there. Though the threadbare pink chairs in the waiting area were unoccupied, the narrow hallway seemed a safer place to be. I was hemmed in on all sides by crisp medical posters and stock photos of water lilies.

Loud thoughts, twitches, and zaps plagued my every move. Terrified and riveted by the battle, which I knew was only beginning to unfold, I felt the urge to urinate. But there was no way I was going to the washroom alone in the midst of all this. Wetness suddenly hit the inside of my thigh. A small puddle was forming by my feet. I took a few steps, watching it trail me. I squeezed my thighs together in an attempt to stem the flow.

See! See! You are crazy!

The thoughts mocked me.

"Aaisha? Hi, my name is Dr. Robyn. I'm a resident working on this floor." A petite young woman with perfectly applied eyeliner was coming to shake my hand.

Res-id-ent!
Res-id-ent!
Res-id-ent!

The thoughts whisper-screamed. "Wow, you're lucky. You'll learn a lot today," I muttered, trying to make sure no drips were following me into the exam room.

She opened a door to a small room with an incredible amount of equipment inside. What looked like an optometrist's eye examination chair was against a wall. The presence of a private washroom confirmed that this wasn't a regular exam room.

"Smells awful in here," Dr. Robyn said, making a face as we all assembled in the room. Adam and Zara squeezed in beside the equipment. "Must be from the washroom," she said, giving me a winning smile before pulling the washroom door closed.

I could feel my eyebrows knitting together as I suspected she was secretly saying the smell was because of me. Who did this resident think she was? I needed a real doctor!

"So what brings you here today?" she asked, flashing me another smile.

I unfurrowed my brows. "I think I've been suffering from postpartum depression ever since my miscarriage a few weeks ago, and I've come to get some medication," I announced, trying my best to rein in the twitches so I wouldn't look bizarre.

"I'm sorry to hear that you had a miscarriage and that you've been depressed lately," she said, scanning my file with all the notes. "But you know, depression is actually quite common. In fact, I take antidepressants myself, and I have been taking them since I was sixteen."

My jaw dropped. Pretty Dr. Robyn with her winning smile and grades good enough for medical school was on antidepressants? Looking at her, I couldn't believe I'd waited so long to ask for medication.

"Mind if I do this questionnaire on you?" she asked, pulling out a sheet of paper.

I nodded. This was a first, probably necessary because she was a resident. As I responded to the first couple of statements that she read out, I found myself still trying to fathom the fact that this doctor was on medication for depression. She seemed so calm and *functional*. I couldn't believe it. I wanted to be like her.

"I have blamed myself unnecessarily when things went wrong," she said, reading off the paper.

"No, never," I said. I had no time to blame myself.

"I have been anxious or worried for no good reason," she said, looking up.

"No, never." I had an excellent *reason* for being anxious and worried.

"Wait." I couldn't help but interrupt. "You're going to send me home and tell me I'm fine and handling things well, aren't you? Listen, I don't need you to ask me all these questions. The fact is that I'm sick, and I need medication." I felt terror rising up inside of me at the thought of being sent home, empty-handed. "I've got these scary intrusive thoughts, and I keep seeing these violent images involving my daughter, and I want them to stop!" I said, getting to my feet.

Dr. Robyn nodded her head. "That's all a part of being depressed. As long as you don't feel like stabbing your daughter to death with a knife, it's depression."

Stab Lina!
Stab Lina!
Stab Lina!

The thoughts screamed gleefully, overjoyed at being tossed a bone.

"Why would you say something like that?" I muttered, collapsing into my chair.

"Well, I think a small dose of Effexor would be good to start you off on, but it does have some side effects, and these include ..." Dr. Robyn's mouth moved up and down, in and out.

For some reason, I suddenly saw the thoughts being typed slowly in my mind in Courier font.

Stab Lina!
Stab Lina!
Stab Lina!
A long carver's knife rammed into Lina's chest over and over again, with a force so great that between each stab, her body jolted up into a semi-seated position.

"I don't care about the side effects," I said, shoving myself right into the doctor's face. "I want some medication right now!" I had no time for this lecture about side effects, not when I could see my daughter being butchered before my eyes.

"I'll go talk to my supervisor," she announced, giving me an alarmed look and rushing out the door.

I paced the room. Lights and sirens were going off in my head, like they were alerting me to the danger of my own self. A cacophony of sounds and images were enveloping me from within, relentlessly. They wouldn't stop unless or until I did something — anything.

The window. The solitary window in the right corner of the room caught my eye.

Jump!
Jump!
Jump!

The thoughts shouted exultingly. Their jubilance made me feel that jumping from the window was what I needed to do to finally make it all stop.

"What are you doing?" Adam asked, rushing over to where I stood trying to pry open the window.

"I need air," I said, only revealing part of why I wanted the window open.

Jump!

Zara and Adam both tried to help, but it was no use. The window was rusted shut. I paced, shaking my head. I was unable to do the one thing I knew could stop the screaming, stabbing, sirens, and lights. I suddenly found my head on Adam's chest. He folded me into himself tightly. For a brief moment, I felt contained and controlled, safe. I closed my eyes.

They flew open at the sound of the door. Dr. Robyn stood with Dr. Bloom. I knew Dr. Bloom; she had been the one who delivered Lina.

"I need some medication!" I screamed, breaking free from Adam's hold. "Inject me with it, stick it in me," I shrieked, thrusting the back of my hand in her face. I needed an IV drip to control the madness. "Just do it to me!"

"She wasn't like this moments ago," Dr. Robyn said, clutching her clipboard to her chest.

"Do it to me," I continued, wondering why the IV drip wasn't already inserted. I felt a hand clutch my own before I heard the words.

"We can't. We don't have anything like that here," Dr. Bloom said in a calm but stern voice.

"I'm giving you this prescription," she said, turning my hand over and placing a small piece of paper into it. She closed my fingers over it.

"I want you to get it filled now and take it. Come back and see me in half an hour, when you are a bit calmer."

· · ·

We all stumbled out of the clinic onto the street. "I'll go get this prescription filled and meet you back here," Zara said, running ahead. Adam was holding tightly to my hand, giving it occasional squeezes.

The cool fall breeze hit me in the face, bringing me back momentarily to the reality of what was around me. People in smart outfits, firmly gripping briefcases, raced to work. Couples crossed the clinic's busy downtown street on their way to appointments. Pregnant women waddled to their monthly appointments. One such woman, with a baby bump that looked about four months along, was walking directly toward me.

Sadness welled up inside at the realization that if not for the miscarriage, I too would have been that far along myself by now.

Don't be sad, just take a knife and slit her belly open. Then, she won't be pregnant anymore and you won't be sad.
A hand gripping a carver's knife plunged into taut pregnant flesh.

My mouth dropped open as I realized that I was being propelled toward the woman. Tears streamed down my face. I didn't want to hurt this woman or harm her in any way. It was the Devil; he was doing this to me. Fast, shallow breathing escaped me.

"I wanna cross the street," I gasped.

Adam steered me away from her as we crossed.

What was going on in my head? Was the Devil already in control, making me think and do things I didn't want to do? "I seek refuge in God, from Satan the accursed," I mumbled repeatedly as I walked. I needed God to win this round, but the Devil was clearly gaining the upper hand.

Couples, irritatingly in-love couples walking aimlessly, were blocking my path on the bustling sidewalk. I needed them to move out of my way.

Just shove them onto the street into oncoming traffic.

My shoulders lurched forward as I felt compelled to make it happen. My breathing grew laboured as I fought against myself. I did not want to kill people. Why wasn't Adam gripping me more tightly? It was hard to resist the urge without help, his help, any help.

If you take a life, it's like you've killed all of humanity. And if you save a life, it's like you've saved all of humanity.

My favourite verse from the Quran filled my mind. The intersection loomed ahead, and I felt my body being driven to thrust myself into the traffic so that I could die. So that I could save lives by not killing anyone else. But at the same time, I didn't want to die. Paradoxical thoughts surrounded me, bewildering me.

"I have it!" I heard Zara exclaim. Adam turned suddenly, forcing me to do a 180 from the intersection I was being pushed toward. I let out a sigh as relief washed over me at escaping the urges momentarily.

"Here," Zara said, placing a solitary pink pill in my hand. Shakily, she handed me a bottle of water.

Please God, help me, I prayed, gulping the pill down. I walked, thinking about the urges. The one from the Devil made sense, as he was evil and would want me to kill people. But who was it that wanted me to kill myself? It couldn't be God. God wasn't like that, but it wasn't from me either. I didn't want to kill myself or anyone else. I wanted to live, but the urges were strong, stronger than me, and it was hard not to succumb to them.

It felt like lead was slowly being poured into every inch of my body, starting with my feet. With each new step, I was lifting a mountain of bricks.

"I can't walk anymore," I said breathlessly.

"That's fine. It's time to go back to see the doc," Zara said.

Sandwiched between Adam and Zara, unable to walk on my own, we headed back to Dr. Bloom.

• • •

"Excuse me, sorry, but we need you to leave this room," I heard a voice say as we walked down the corridor. "This lady really needs to be in here." Outlines of bodies shuffled out of a room while a lone figure motioned us in. Larger than the previous one, this room had a desk, chairs, and an examination table. I noted that the window was larger and that it was open.

"So, how do you feel now?" Dr. Bloom asked, seating herself so she could look directly at me. Her glasses sat perched on her nose. Her voice was slow, calming, and soothing, like the waves of an ocean.

"Slow and heavy," I said, trying my best not to slur my words.

Cuuuuuut oooooooff heeeeer fffface wwwwwith a kkkkknife.

I glanced away, unable to look into her eyes. The thought was painfully slow, but the last thing I wanted to do was take a knife to this gentle woman's face. Not only because she was a human being, but because she was the one who'd help bring Lina into this world.

"Yes, that's because you were having a panic attack before. I gave you a high dose of Klonopin to calm you down," she continued, trying to catch my eye again.

Cuuuuuut oooooooff heeeeer fffface wwwwwith a kkkkknniffe.

I looked away uncomfortably. The urge was there, but because of my newfound heaviness, the fear that I might actually be capable of acting on it wasn't very strong.

"I'm prescribing you an antidepressant, Effexor, and an anti-anxiety medication, Klonopin. They should make you feel better," she said, scribbling on her pad.

"But will they make the thoughts and feelings go away?"

"Well, not *right* away, but soon."

"I believe in the sanctity of life," I started. "All life, including mine." I thought of all the evil urges. I wanted to lay the foundation of who I was as a person before I told her the monstrous truth.

She nodded understandingly, like she was silently affirming that she did know I was a good person.

"But when I went outside, I felt like doing bad things to people. And then, because I didn't want to do bad things to other people, I felt like doing bad things to myself."

"What kind of bad things?" she asked gently, leaning in.

"They're evil," I said, shaking my head. I couldn't, or wouldn't, tell her. They were things that should never be spoken of. I recalled the urge to slice the pregnant woman's belly, push unsuspecting people to their death, and throw myself into the street.

"I want to be locked up," I said, certain that it was the only way to keep others safe. To keep them safe from me, and me safe from myself.

She straightened up suddenly. Shocked glances were being shared around the room, which was filled to capacity. Adam and Zara stood near the open window, and Dr. Bloom sat across from me at her desk. Huddled by the door were Dr. Robyn, one nurse I recognized from before, and another one who was new.

"Well, that will be a bit of a problem," Dr. Bloom said. "There's no psychiatrist on call, so I'll have to call the police to arrange that."

What she was saying didn't make sense to me, but I knew that in a roundabout way she was saying no.

"I think you can go home," she said. "Especially if people promise to stay with you and watch you." She looked around for agreement.

I shook my head. It was a bad idea, but Adam and Zara were nodding vigorously.

"How about I leave you guys to discuss it," she said, getting up to depart. My audience shuffled out, leaving Adam, Zara, and me alone in the room.

"I want to be locked up," I said, looking down as tears splashed on my hands.

"You need to come home with us," Adam said.

I shook my head again. I needed help to stop myself from giving into the battle in my mind. I was weak and couldn't trust myself not to give in.

"Please, we'll watch you. Even I can help," Zara said pleadingly. She was crouched before me, holding my hands and trying to get me to look at her. She was so sweet. If she only knew what a monster I was, she wouldn't dare offer to be anywhere near me.

I kept shaking my head.

"It'll be easier for your parents and Lina," Adam said. "Downtown is so far away from where they live."

My mom's haggard face came into my head. The vision of her collapsing into Zara's arms as I'd climbed into the car flashed in front of me. I stopped shaking my head, realizing I had put my family through enough already.

Zara jumped to her feet. "I'll tell the doctor."

"So she's decided to come home with us," Adam said.

"Great news. I just need to know one thing," Dr. Bloom said, planting herself across from me again. "But you need to look at me first." I looked at her.

Cuuuuuut ooooooff heeeeer fffface

"I need to know, are you safe?"

I thought about her question. It loomed large in my mind, like the "make-it-or-break-it" question it was. I thought about the urges and loud thoughts, about how they were so painfully slow. I also thought about how the urges felt less dangerous now, because of how heavy I felt.

"Will I always feel this heavy because of the medication?" I asked slowly. My words felt like they were crawling out of my mouth. Even asking that one question was exhausting.

"Yes, I think so," she said. "It's because I gave you such a large dose compared to your body size," she said, a little apologetically. "Once I refer you to a psychiatrist, he or she can figure out a proper dose for you," she added.

"Ok," I said, sighing. "I'm safe."

It would be so much easier to believe that what had happened to me here, being dangerously misdiagnosed, was atypical — that it was some unusual aberration that would not regularly occur.

The grim reality is that racialized women, who already experience higher rates of postpartum mood disorders, are more likely than their white counterparts to be misdiagnosed. At least one study found that Indian women like me, with postpartum mood disorders, were more likely to be misdiagnosed than diagnosed properly.[1] This can have devastating implications.

Perhaps what best illustrates the potential tragedy of a misdiagnosis is the story of Otty Sanchez. Sanchez was a new mother with a history of mental-health issues who was diagnosed with postpartum depression after the birth of her son, Scotty. On July 20, 2009, she found herself at her local hospital in San Antonio, Texas.[2] It is documented that she was delusional and experiencing auditory and visual hallucinations at the time. Despite requesting to be admitted, Sanchez was released to the care of her family. Any woman experiencing hallucinations or delusions (which are both indicative of psychosis) in the postpartum period should be immediately hospitalized.

Within six days of being sent home, three-week-old Scotty was killed during his mother's severe psychotic episode.[3] Sanchez had also tried unsuccessfully to take her own life and was found weeping that the Devil made her do it.

Had she received inpatient care rather than being sent home, this tragedy would never have occurred. It wasn't the Devil that made her do it. It was more likely the devil in the details of a system that allows women who are experiencing psychosis, particularly women of colour, to be sent home to care for their infants.

17: HIDE THE KNIVES

A CAKE BEARING THE WORDS "WELCOME BACK" IN curly pink icing waited for me on a table surrounded by Lina, my parents, my siblings, and their kids. A party was in full swing commemorating my return, either from the doctor or from the land of insanity — I wasn't sure which. Family members with their plates piled with veggie rolls and samosas passed by, flashing me the occasional grin. Perched on the edge of the sofa, I sat with my own plate of delicacies, an awkward smile plastered on my face.

Despite the festive atmosphere, I couldn't get the thoughts, images, and urges out of my head. Why did it feel like I was at risk of giving in to the violent thoughts and urges from the Devil? Was it a testament to the fact that I was a bad person?

"Am I a good person?" I asked my dad, leaning across the sofa we were sharing. He was carefully dunking a samosa into tamarind chutney. He looked up, caught off guard, and broke into a wide smile.

"What kind of question is that, sweetie? Of course you're a good person!" He finished off his samosa, shaking his head at the apparent silliness of my question.

I kept at it, catching different people as they went about their business and forcing them to sit, so I could ask them the only question that mattered. "Am I a good person?" Chuckles and pats on the head did little to quell the knot building in my chest, making me feel that, maybe, I was not a good person.

Hours later, arms were pulling a crying, kicking Lina away from me. "Mommy can't sleep with you, because my legs are filled with something really heavy," I said, trying to explain why we couldn't sleep together. Even if we couldn't play anymore, joining me in bed was her one respite since we'd come to my mom's over three weeks ago. "Your body will get stuck under my legs." Sadness welled up inside at what I was doing to Lina, but I knew it had to be done.

"She'll be fine," Adam said, sitting beside me on the bed. "I'm taking time off from work to be with you and her."

"Hide the knives," I said, looking at him conspiratorially.

"What? Why?"

"Just hide them," I said. I was safe from giving into the Devil's violent urges during the day. Even if he forced me, I was sure that my slow, now-medicated movements could easily be stopped by practically anyone. I wasn't so sure about it at night, however. I could just see myself being compelled against my will by the Devil to slowly lumber down the stairs, get a knife, and slaughter everyone as they slept.

I fell asleep before I could find out if Adam did my bidding.

• • •

"Three people were shot yesterday." My eyes snapped open. The radio continued to blare violence at me.

"Turn it off, turn it off!" I screamed, now fully awake.

"What? What's wrong?" Adam asked, scurrying to hit the off button. Rapid breaths consumed me. I wondered what new compilation of gruesome sounds, images, and urges the Devil would put together on a mixtape for me.

Over the next few days, moving around the house became progressively easier as the Devil's power over me strengthened. I couldn't understand why the Devil was consistently getting the upper hand over God. Maybe it wasn't God's fault but my own weakness.

Adam, my dad, and even my mom became exasperated at my constant restriction of what they were allowed to speak about. Any mention of violence happening in the world was totally forbidden around me. I banned certain words, even in contexts unrelated to violence, like "hang," "knife," and "shovel." Those were no-nos because they could potentially inspire the Devil to plant violent thoughts or images in my head.

"Hi Dr. Bloom," I heard Adam saying into the phone about three days into my Klonopin and Effexor treatment. "She's doing a lot better."

"I need to speak to her," I said, tripping over myself in my hurried attempt to snatch the phone.

"Dr. Bloom?" I said breathlessly. "I need more Klonopin. I'm not feeling as slow or heavy anymore, like you promised." This was dire. The slowness and heaviness were my crutches, what I was relying on to ward off the Devil's urges.

"You're probably developing tolerance to it. But you're already on the maximum dose for your body size. I can't safely give you more," she said. "But I wanted to tell you, I got you an appointment with a psychiatrist on Thursday at 2 p.m. Maybe she will be able to add something to help. Take care. Bye."

My face crumpled at the terrifying prospect of losing my ammunition to fight back against the Devil. Three whole days of waiting to see the psychiatrist seemed like a lifetime.

I could hear the din from the office adjacent to where I sat. The soft sofas were a contrast to the speckled industrial linoleum tiles beneath my feet. A long hallway punctuated by white doors on each side faced me. Posters reminding me about the importance of a "check up from the neck up" seemed to frown down at me from walls.

"Reproductive Mental Health Department. How can I help?" The woman's voice kept repeating the same thing every time the phone rang. Her voice was high and kept yanking me out of the stupor I was in.

"Aaisha?" A tall, slim woman wearing a crisp navy pantsuit with her hair in a feathery brown bob stood eyeing me from about six feet away. Adam shot up, while I rose slowly. "My name is Dr. Baker," she said, offering me a hand.

I reached forward at a snail's pace to grip it weakly. I began my never-ending shuffle from the cozy comfort of the waiting room, down the long hallway to her office. Dr. Baker seemed in a rush, and I couldn't keep up with her long legs.

"Usually, is she a little slow?" she said quizzically, standing in front of her office waiting for me to make it.

Anger made a slow climb to my head as I realized what she was implying. I couldn't wait to let her have it. "I'm smmmmmm-maaaaarttt," I heard myself snarl. "IIIIIII hhaaaaaavveeee muuuuullllitttppple deeeegrreeeees," I said, even before settling into the chair awaiting me.

Redness flooded across her chiseled face. "That's not what I meant. You were moving so slowly," she said, hastily trying to backtrack.

I wasn't sure I liked this woman.

Questions about everything from my childhood to my relationship with Adam were covered in quick succession. I could feel the wheels in my brain turning slowly, agonizingly, to string coherent answers together. After that barb about being "slow," I *needed* to show her that I was intelligent and articulate. But despite my best efforts, I didn't sound clever, because of how long it took for things to creep out of my mouth. Sadly, my old vocabulary was out of reach in this version of me.

I took in the room. I'd never been in a psychiatrist's office before. It seemed unusually bland. The clean desk where she was seated, the two chairs Adam and I were seated in, and a small shelf with some books. Where was the couch that I was supposed to be lying on?

"How were you after your first pregnancy?" she asked, pen poised to continue with her notes.

"I think I had postpartum depression then," I said slowly.

"Why do you say that?" she asked, lips pursed.

"Because I was sad and miserable. Then, I used to have this scary thought of my baby's fontanel being pierced with an iron handrail," I said, embarrassment colouring my voice. "Because I was scared of it, I wanted to give her up for adoption. I also thought my family would harm her. I kept thinking she wasn't really a baby and that she was doing things on purpose."

"What did you take to get better?" she asked, jolting up in her seat like I'd just confessed to something monumental.

"Nothing. One day I just woke up and realized that none of that stuff was true."

She scribbled furiously, before looking up again. "What are your symptoms this time?"

"Sadness, exhaustion, scary thoughts and images," I replied. I couldn't possibly tell her about God and the Devil battling for my mind or that I knew the Devil was putting images in my head. *That part* was true. I knew it wasn't part of the illness. Telling her about that would only confuse her and make her think I was delusional.

"Do you want to hurt yourself or others?" she asked.

I could feel my eyebrows shooting up, even in slow motion. Why was she asking me this? What did she suspect?

"No," I said resolutely. Though I did have terrifying thoughts and violent urges, they were not things I *wanted* to do, they were things I was actively *not* wanting to do.

"If you take a life, it's like you've killed all of humanity, and if you save life, it's like you've saved all of humanity," I said, quoting from the Quran. "I believe in the sanctity of life, all life, including mine," I continued, making sure to set the record straight.

I saw her scribbling something down and hoped it was my words about how I abhorred violence.

"Do you think people are watching you?"

Where was she going with these questions? "No," I scoffed. It wasn't like I was paranoid or delusional.

Shuffling her papers together, she pursed her lips again, like she was on the verge of a bold pronouncement. "I'm really worried your mind is starting to play tricks on you. I want you to triple your dose of Effexor and reduce your Klonopin to half."

My heart skipped a beat. I needed the Klonopin to weigh me down and stop me from giving in to the urges.

"I also want to start you on a new class of medication," she said crisply.

"Are you going to start me on antipsychotics?" I asked.

"Yes, yes," she said approvingly, sounding excited that I knew about such drugs. "I want to put you on Seroquel," she said.

My face crumpled, and I could barely get my words out. "You're hurting my feelings by saying I'm psychotic," I said, gulping tearfully. I felt like she was stamping the words LIFE OVER on my forehead.

"No, I'm not saying you're psychotic," she said, scrambling to course correct. "Real psychotic people need so much of this," she said, thrusting her prescription pad at me. "This is such a small dose, it's really more of a tranquilizer."

The image of a humongous, thrashing wild elephant needing to be sedated to stop it from harming villagers entered my mind.

"Look, you are not psychotic, *yet*," she said. "You're not hallucinating, paranoid, or delusional, but I don't want you to get to that point. It seems like you had psychotic features to your depression the first time around, and I don't want it to get like that again. I want to stave off a dangerous psychotic episode."

Oh, oh, Adam's gonna leave you for sure now!

This time I felt confident the thought was right. "Now it's gonna be *your* fault when Adam leaves me, once I get fat," I said, remembering how I'd read that weight gain was a known side effect of some antipsychotics. I shook my head, convinced he finally had a real reason to leave me.

Dr. Baker's eyebrows shot up as she looked over at Adam. He threw his hands up, confused, like he had no clue what I was talking about. As if, I thought. He'd never before expressed a problem with my weight. Actually, he was the one always shoving Cinnabons and treats on me. Still, the thoughts couldn't be wrong. They probably knew something he and I didn't.

"If you hear voices, see things, or want to harm yourself or anyone else, go to the emergency room," she stressed. "And you," she said, turning to Adam. "You need to make sure she's being watched at all times, and is never alone."

She handed me a box of tissues. As I got to my feet, I knew already that there weren't enough in the box.

• • •

"So, I heard the bad news," Idris said on the phone.

I sniffled. Even he knew my life was over.

"It's hard to believe you're a *psychopath*," he whispered.

"What? I'm not a psychopath. I'm just a little psychotic," I said, feeling woozy.

"Sorry, but that's what Mom and Dad told me," he said, discomfort evident in his voice.

"'Psychotic' means you're not in touch with reality. A psychopath is like Ted Bundy," I said. This call couldn't be over fast enough. I hung up the phone.

18: SIXTH SENSE

ZARA HELD OPEN THE DOOR, WELCOMING ME INTO her home the next day. The week had been long and taxing on my mom and Adam. I was being shuffled to Zara's place to give them a well-deserved break. I headed straight for her blue corduroy sofa. The early afternoon sun's rays seemed to illuminate it with a halo of light. I idly watched the rays do a little dance on the glass doors of the fireplace every time the blinds fluttered.

As afternoon turned to night, the inviting warmth of her family room was offset by the corpses.

Corpses dangling from her ceiling.

It looked almost like a scene from *The Sixth Sense*, the last movie Adam and I had rented before I fell ill, except I knew that it wasn't. This was God's work, giving me a glimpse of Hell. And Hell apparently consisted of black and white old-timey people in pioneer clothing paying for their sins. Any sense of horror was replaced by awe at what God was choosing to reveal to me. Later that evening, my family arrived. Adam was going to fill them in on what was going on with me and go over the medications I needed.

"She has to take three Effexors, one Klonopin, and one Seroquel a day," Adam said, rattling off the list on his piece of paper. "She's gonna stay with Zara and Mariya for the next five days, then come back to Mom's place with me. I know this will probably mean my contract won't be renewed, but I am taking time off work to help care for her and Lina. That is non-negotiable."

There was a swift turning of heads and hushed angry muttering. It didn't matter, I thought. There were more important issues to address.

It was now my turn. "What's happening to me is very frightening," I started. Everyone nodded.

"There are corpses everywhere," I said, motioning to the ceiling.

Startled looks were being exchanged, but I knew what the problem was. My family couldn't see them; only I could. "God is showing me what Hell looks like, so I can tell you all," I said. "So I can warn you all to fix your lives. Fix them before it's too late!" I warned ominously.

After that, there was a private meeting between my parents and Adam that I wasn't allowed into. Nevertheless I felt better, knowing that thanks to my warning, everyone left that evening a little more aware of their need to redeem themselves.

• • •

I shut my eyes.

> *A metal pipe, hollow but at the same time, occupied. A furry black and red sock inchworming its way through the piping. Creeping, inching, creeping, inching.*
> *"Peek-a-boo," it screamed, eyeless.*

"I need to go to the hospital," I said, breathless and trembling at what I'd just seen. Even though my eyes were closed, it seemed real, not a thought but an actual vision. Mariya and Zara, who were hunched over a magazine on the same king-size bed as me, sat up surprised. This sock vision was scarier than almost everything else because I couldn't tell whether this was a message from God or the Devil, or what it meant. The fact that I couldn't make out who sent me the message bothered me the most. Was this insanity?

I was confident I needed to go to the hospital. "Guys, call the ambulance, please." I didn't want to tell them what I'd seen. It was far too horrifying. But they pressed me, promising to take me after I told them what was wrong.

I described my vision for them.

"Here, take your Klonopin," Mariya said, depositing a pill into my hand.

"But I have to go to the hospital. Dr. Baker told me to go if I start seeing things."

"We'll take you, after you swallow this," she said, forcing a glass of water on me.

I fell asleep.

• • •

The following day, Mariya and Zara took me to the mall to boost my spirits. Accompanying them was the least I could do, considering how much time they'd taken off to care for me.

We walked into the Gap, ready to bargain hunt and rifle through the clearance racks. Music drifted out of the speakers.

Shoot, punch, kick

PART 3

I froze midway through eyeing a frilly top Mariya was holding up. I couldn't believe his audacity. The Devil was trying to speak to me, albeit surreptitiously, through the music. He was saying things I didn't want to hear. Fingers firmly planted in my ears, I made a run for it.

I paced outside the store, shaking my head at his boldness. What if others heard him? It was like he didn't even care to keep the battle a secret anymore.

"The music is bothering me," I said, when Mariya and Zara caught up, wondering where I'd run off to. No matter how many different stores we went to, I heard him take over the music to talk to me. I couldn't believe how quickly and effectively the Devil had turned the mall into his personal playground.

Because I clearly wanted to stay away from the individual stores, Zara and Mariya stuck to the middle of the mall, checking out the different kiosks.

Stacks of glimmering containers in gem-like colours filled the booth, testifying to the current "mineral makeup" craze. I feigned interest as the vendor explained how the same powdered mineral could be used in different ways to make lipstick, eyeshadow, and blush. Truthfully, I was just happy the guy couldn't play music out of his little cart. Believing it was the makeup itself that had me captivated, Mariya and Zara dropped a small fortune on it, promising me a makeover to remember.

• • •

Back at Zara's, her master bathroom was swiftly converted into an impromptu makeup studio. Tiny shimmering vials in a rainbow of powdered hues lined the counter, alongside jars of Q-tips, makeup wipes, and brushes.

Perched on a stool, I sat with my back to the long mirror while one pair of deft hands worked swiftly to pencil in, brush on, and expertly apply the minerals. The other pair worked my hair, trying to magically transform curly tangles into glamor.

"You are not going to recognize yourself when we're done!" Mariya exclaimed.

Half an hour later, it was time for the big reveal. Getting to my feet with my eyes closed, I felt hands on my shoulders, turning me around.

"Open your eyes!" they squealed eagerly.

A kaleidoscope of exaggerated facial features highlighted in garish colours stared back at me. I gasped. Was that the Devil looking at me?

"I don't like it. I don't like it. I'm scared!" I shrieked back. Glimmer and shimmer swirled down the sink. The Devil had even managed to take over a makeup session.

· · ·

"He hasn't called or visited in three days," I said. I was lying on the corduroy sofa that had grown to be my loyal companion.

"He's probably busy with Lina," Mariya said.

"No time for even a call?" I said dejectedly, rolling over so that nobody could see my tears welling up.

"Look who's here!" Zara announced about an hour later, opening the door to a grinning Adam.

"Hey, you," he said, coming over to me. I turned away. Tears splashed onto my dependable corduroy companion. "What's wrong?" he asked, sitting on the little bit of blue space beside me.

"What's wrong? What's wrong?" I said, flopping over so he could see me. "You're wrong! You haven't called or visited in three days," I cried, unable to control the flood.

"I'm sorry," he said, scrambling to his feet. "I was mad."

"Mad? Mad at what?" He wasn't making any sense.

"Mad about the scene that happened when your family came over," he said.

I didn't know what he was talking about. All I'd done was warn them about what Hell was like. You'd think he'd thank me, not stonewall me. "I hate you," I said, thinking about how he'd left me to fend for myself with the furry sock and devilish face in the mirror. "I hate you more than anything in this world!"

"Fine," he said, turning on his heel and walking away. "I'm going. Good luck with your new caregivers!" he yelled, before slamming the door.

I felt myself falling, falling from a tall, spiralling staircase. Falling was bad enough, but I couldn't bear to contemplate who or what was waiting for me at the bottom. "No, don't go!" I screamed, bolting from my blue sofa.

Thwack. I ran smack into Mariya, who was blocking the door. I punched her and she buckled over, gripping her stomach as I escaped through the entrance.

Adam scowled, getting into our car. "Let's get you back in," Zara said, gripping one of my hands while Mariya clasped the other.

• • •

I lay on the corduroy sofa again, feeling miserable and frightened by what my life had become. It was bad enough that Adam had been stonewalling me because he was mad, but what was my little brother's excuse? Though everyone else had come for the family meeting, Idris was MIA, which was too bad, because he could have really benefited from my sage advice. I loved and missed him, but I was also angry at him for not bothering to visit. I wanted to see his smiling face and be reminded of the good old days, back when we were best buds as kids.

Don't be sad. If he comes, just take a knife and cut
off his head. Then you can always see him.
Idris's decapitated head sat staring at me with a
sloppy smile.

I cried softly to myself, rolling over so no one could see me. I couldn't believe the lengths the Devil was going to to make me do his bidding.

"You said you would come out for Chinese food," Mariya said, sitting on the blue of the sofa. There was more of the couch available, as I was sitting up, trying to catch a glimpse of the inkiness of the night through the gap in the blinds.

"What are you staring at?" Zara said, coming to whip the blinds apart.

Ghostly white trees stared back at me. Their barren
branches ready.

My eyes widened with horror. I gulped, knowing what was to come. The Devil was going to hang all the corpses on the ghostly limbs of the trees, like Christmas ornaments.

"I don't want to go anymore!" I yelled, flopping back on my sofa. How could I explain anything to them without divulging the reality of the secret battle between God and the Devil?

"But why?" Mariya asked, perplexed.

"Because I *don't*." Would they want to go out if they knew the Devil was going to try to speak to them? I rolled over. This was my test, and my test alone.

The following morning was better. Rough brown-barked trees stared back at me through the window. I lay on my blue sofa, content.

Jiggle. Squinting, I stared hard at the ceiling. Did the ceiling actually jiggle? No. It was shivering. I looked away, lowering my gaze to the wall below; it undulated. I closed my eyes to get away from the madness of it all.

"How about some soup?" Mariya said, balancing a trembling bowl. I shut my eyes.

"Come on, you have to eat. You've been lying on this sofa for too long, not eating or talking." Methodical stirring was punctuated by the occasional sound of falling liquid.

"Here," she said.

Hunger filled my belly, so I opened my eyes and sat up. Two dents atop a long slash marked the undulating wall behind my sister. *Wink.*

I recoiled at the realization that the wall had winked at me. *First it'll be pots, then kettles. They'll all start talking to you.* I remembered the talking cow's ominous pronouncement from my dream in the early days, when I first got sick. It was materializing before my very eyes.

"Just leave me alone," I said as Mariya brought the jiggling spoon toward me. I rolled over, tears streaming onto the couch.

I was officially in another dimension, and I knew it. I had merged into a realm that even Salvador Dali's surrealist paintings of melted clocks couldn't do justice to. Terror gripped me at the possibility that I might actually be able to see the Devil now that I'd crossed over to this new dimension. To ward that off for as long as I could, I decided to spend the bulk of my time lying down with my eyes shut tightly.

That I was in a new dimension was proven by the fact that even the most mundane items in Zara's house would move in bizarre ways. Crisp apples would stand on legs, carrots topped with sprigs of greenery would twirl and tango, and plates and spoons would tap dance, flashing me the occasional smile. But at least these events would happen only when my eyes were closed. Or were they closed? I couldn't be sure. What did it matter anyway?

• • •

"Come. You need to take a bath," I heard a familiar voice say. I opened one eye to take a peek to see if it was really true. My mom stood before me, hands hanging at her side, looking better than I'd seen her in weeks.

"No, I don't want to." I shuddered at the thought of the Devil in the bathroom alone with me.

"But you haven't bathed in two weeks."

Big deal. They wouldn't have time to bathe either if they were privy to all the realities that I was privy to.

"You'll see how much better you'll feel. Come now."

"Will you stay in the washroom with me while I shower?" I asked, suddenly changing tack and making a move to get up. I knew the Devil wouldn't dare reveal himself while someone else was around.

"Okay," she said. I leapt off my sofa.

Hot water striking my body felt relaxing and comforting, but it wasn't enough. I needed to fling open and close the shower curtain rapidly, to make sure my mom was staying put so the Devil knew I wasn't alone. I couldn't help but feel pleased at how I'd outwitted him.

• • •

The constant undulating of my surroundings kept me alert for the imminent arrival of the Devil. Creases on the walls kept morphing to get the Devil's words out to me. Those words would no doubt be even more horrifying things I didn't want to hear. I'd never asked to be privy to all of this. I felt like I could use some help in coping with this new reality God was exposing me to. Would more Klonopin help?

Unfortunately, in my mind I wasn't experiencing any of the things that would necessitate a trip to the emergency room — hearing voices, seeing things others couldn't, or wanting to harm others. Sure, I was seeing things others couldn't, but that was because I'd entered a new reality. Also, I never *wanted* to harm anyone; I was being forced to think of doing so against my will.

Nothing made this clearer than the newest image I was beset with: a serrated knife drawing itself against my own throat. It would pop up right after any of the violent thoughts or images, which, courtesy of the Devil, were frequent. This knife image served as a healing balm, an offer of an easy way out of the madness my life had turned into.

19: THE DIVA
YOU ARE

AFTER NEARLY A WEEK, I WENT BACK TO MY MOM'S house with Adam. I lay with my head on his lap, wrapped in my dad's cozy blue blanket. Sadness welled up in me as I considered what my life had become. Plus, I missed my corduroy couch at Zara's.

"Don't be sad, we love you," said a woman's voice. I whipped off the blanket, looking around to see who had uttered the words.

"Whoa!" said Adam, reacting to my abrupt movement.

This was the last straw. I had finally become insane. I had heard a woman's voice, and I knew it wasn't God or the Devil. The Devil didn't love me, and I was sure God wouldn't sound like some random woman.

"I need to call Dr. Baker," I said, running to the phone. I wanted to tell her before I went to the hospital.

"Dr. Baker? It's me, Aaisha. I heard a voice in my head," I said breathlessly, thinking about how I'd finally turned the bend — lost it — gone over the edge.

"Take a breath," she said. "Tell me what happened."

"I was lying under a blanket, then I heard a lady's voice say, 'Don't be sad, we love you.'" I was confident she would send the ambulance over to take me away.

"Were you awake or asleep when that happened?"

What kind of a question was that? I'd heard a voice, wasn't that good enough?

"Maybe asleep?" I wasn't sure, and I didn't want to mess up.

"I want you to take another Seroquel, so take two a day, and come see me the day after tomorrow at two thirty."

No ambulances arrived.

• • •

"Reproductive Mental Health Department. How can I help?" I waited until the small, owlish woman behind the desk was done before letting her know I'd arrived.

"Two-thirty appointment with Dr. Baker," I said.

"Please wait next door and she'll get you," she said. I couldn't tell if she was talking to me or into her headset. I assumed correctly and hurried to the U-shaped couches in the next room. For a weathered hospital that looked like it had been around long enough to serve the needs of Anne of Green Gables herself, it had a smart contemporary interior. Gray streamlined sofas, which I knew were more comfortable than they looked, sat surrounding a nondescript coffee table with an array of magazines with articles like "How to Have Incredible Sex" and "Hosting Like the Diva You Are." I stared at them, unable to decide which magazine was better to have in my hands in order to look less like a mental-health patient.

"You okay?" Adam asked. I nodded. I needed to go over my script of what to say.

"Aaisha?" Dr. Baker called from down the hallway. I noticed she was being lazy, not bothering to set foot near the waiting area this time, so I hurried to meet her.

She smiled. "Hey, you're not as slow today."

I sat down across from her as Adam huddled in his seat.

"So, how are you today?"

"I think I'm a little better," I said, recalling that I hadn't felt the terrifying urges since I'd called her. My other problem, how I had merged with the wobbly dimension where the Devil was waiting, crept into my head. I wished I could tell her my secret sadness, but she wasn't Muslim and would never understand.

"I'm really anxious," I said, confessing to the real *medical* issue she could help me with. I needed help in addressing my fear of this new dimension. I'd always had a nervous disposition as a child, which had earned me the nickname "worrywart." I could see now how appropriate that was.

"I have a fear of violent words. They trigger violent imagery."

She nodded sympathetically. She wasn't as bad as the first day I'd met her. She seemed far more relaxed and less commanding. The fact that she wasn't wearing a banker's suit like she had the first time also made her look more chill.

"I want you to increase your Seroquel. Take two at night and up to three during the day over the next couple of days, and halve your Klonopin."

I left. I didn't care anymore that I was taking more of the "elephant tranquilizer." If it would help me cope with my new reality, I would down the whole bottle.

• • •

"What are you doing?" Adam said, resting his chin on my shoulder.

"I'm writing out the Quran," I said, trying to make out the blur of words on the page.

"Why?"

"It brings me comfort," I said, looking up mid squint. Well, at least I hoped it would bring me comfort. A gnawing feeling had been growing in the pit of my stomach. I now felt like I needed to — no, *had* to — write out passages of the Quran if I wanted God's help.

I'd been initially eager to give it a go. But as the hours passed, I grew weary, especially because I couldn't make out the words with my blurry vision. Seroquel was apparently notorious for that, according to the medication leaflet.

But still, copying the words onto ten big legal-size sheets every day was what it would take to qualify for God's mercy.

"But everything is already written down in the Quran!" Adam would say when he saw me exhausted, trying to rub the bleariness from my eyes as I sat hunched over my sheafs of paper. It seemed pointless to explain.

· · ·

After three hours copying out ten long pages, I dragged myself to bed. I had done a total of thirty pages over the past three days, but each new day's work took longer than the previous day's.

"I think the extra meds are helping," Adam said as I lay down beside him.

I frowned. It was upsetting that he couldn't see that my improvement was directly connected to copying out the pages of the Quran. We spooned in bed like I loved.

"Say the F-word to Him."

I flipped over to see if Adam had whispered something, and I'd misheard him.

"What?" Adam said, feeling my gaze even through the darkness.

"Did you say something?" I asked.

"No."

"Okay," I said, rolling back over and closing my eyes.

"Say the F-word to Him," a voice said, louder this time. My eyes jerked open as I realized who it was. It was the Devil.

"No!" I whispered, flipping onto my stomach. I wasn't going to listen to him. I loved God, and He was going to help me through this.

"Say the F-word to Him," he ordered, getting agitated by my defiance.

"No, I won't," I said.

"Say the F-word to Him, right now!" He was enraged at the ridiculousness of a mere mortal daring to stand up to him.

"No!" I heard myself scream. "I won't do it!" I needed to get away from him. I got to my feet.

"What's wrong? What's happening?" I heard Adam say, scrambling to his feet.

"Say the F-word to Him, right now!" the Devil screeched again.

A stark, powdery white face. Ultra-black irises surrounded by white pupils, heavily rimmed with teal. Crimson lips, parted widely to reveal sharpened, rotting teeth.

"*No!*" I screamed, kicking and lashing my fists out at him.

The Devil's face was frozen, gaping mid-screech. I couldn't understand how he was able to talk with his face frozen.

"Get me the pill, get me the pill!" Adam was yelling to someone. I could hear my parents' voices in the background. Adam's arms were wrapped around my waist, pulling me into himself. Why didn't he want me to stop the Devil?

Fingers jammed into my mouth, forcing me to swallow something.

"Is it safe for me to take so many pills?" I heard myself say.

. . .

"I didn't get to finish copying out my verses," I said, stepping into Zara's the next day. The corduroy blue couch sat a little away from the door, but I automatically felt a sense of warmth and comfort. "Can we talk after I finish?"

"Sure, whatever works for you," she said, clearing some space out for me on the dining table.

Was that a *the* or *He*? I couldn't make out the blurred words, so how could I possibly be expected to copy out all these pages? It was like I was being set up to fail. Where was God's mercy? It didn't feel like mercy. What if the feeling that I needed to copy out these verses wasn't from God but was coming from the Devil? He was tricky like that.

"Say the F-word to Him."

I put down my pen. Did Zara hear that? She was bustling over to water the succulents at her kitchen window, undisturbed. If she'd heard an unfamiliar voice, she would have turned, face filled with alarm. She was a chicken like that, easily scared.

"Say the F-word to Him," the Devil repeated.

I knew it wouldn't be long before he started screeching like he did yesterday, and what if he showed up again? I was alone with Zara, wonderful but timid Zara. I needed to keep calm but didn't know how to pull it off.

"Say the F-word to Him," he said again, menacingly. I could feel my breathing coming in short choppy bursts. I was a bad actor.

"What's wrong?" Zara said, coming over.

I didn't want to tell her; it would send her running and leave me alone with him. Who knew what ghastly stuff he would force me to do?

"I need to call my doctor," I said, unable to hide my horror or trembling.

"Say the F-word to Him, right now!"

"I need to call right now," I grabbed the phone off the base and punched in the numbers I'd committed to memory.

"Dr. Baker? This is Aaisha," I started. "He's gonna make me swear at God!" I shrieked into the phone. "He's gonna make me swear at God, and then God's gonna abandon me!" Just hearing the words out loud was enough to break the dam. I couldn't bear the thought of God abandoning me.

"Calm down!" she said, sounding anything but calm herself. "Tell me again what's happening."

"There's a voice," I said, still conscious that I couldn't divulge the secret about the Devil.

"And he's forcing me to say the F-word to God, and I don't wanna say it, because I don't want God to abandon me." My shoulders were shaking, and I felt inconsolable, hopeless. There was nothing anyone could do, short of killing the Devil, that was going to help me.

"Listen to me, Aaisha. None of this, none of what is happening to you is your fault. You are sick. Do you hear me?"

I was sick. I was sick. She was right. I was sick, and God knew better than anyone else that I was sick. He wouldn't abandon me. My breathing began to slow at this realization. God was merciful.

"Now, the voice you're hearing, is it your own voice or someone else's?" It was a weird question to ask. Up until she asked it, I was confident it was someone else's. I replayed the voice in my head, wanting to be entirely accurate. I couldn't believe the result.

"It's actually *my* voice, but a really, really, really angry version of my voice," I said in disbelief. There was no way that voice was mine, even if it did sound like it. It was simply the Devil, tricky as he was, using my screeching voice to amplify what he wanted to say.

But the part about the Devil needed to be kept secret, lest she think that was a delusion, part of my illness.

"I want you to up your Seroquels," she said. "Take another five, so that you're taking a total of ten a day, but increase slowly, adding two more each day. And I want you to up your Effexors by another two. Who's there with you?"

"Zara, my best friend," I said, wondering why this woman couldn't settle on how many of the tranquilizers I needed to take. From one to two, then five, and now ten.

"Give the phone to her," she said.

• • •

"Here," Zara said, handing me some tiny pills. I swallowed them. I took several deep breaths to calm myself. The Seroquels were weird like that. They often made me suddenly become aware of the fact that I'd been sitting in a patch of fog. Whenever I took the little pills, mist that I never noticed before would start to disintegrate before my very eyes. Even the undulating walls would become static. "Magic pills" would have been a more appropriate name for them.

I was confused. The Devil was making me swear at God, but the Devil's voice sounded like an angry version of me. God was merciful, but He was forcing me to copy out verses even when He knew I couldn't see well because of the medication.

None of it made sense.

"I can't figure out who's who!" I finally burst out. "Is God making me copy out the verses, or is it the Devil?" It was too confusing.

"What? What do you mean?" Zara asked, looking even more confused than I felt.

"Who's who?" I said. "Who's making me copy out the verses?"

I could see she didn't understand, thinking I'd been copying out all the verses because it calmed me or lifted my spirits.

"I keep feeling like I have to copy out these verses or I won't get better, but it's so hard to do because the medication makes it hard to see," I said, breaking down at how utterly hopeless the task was. "Is that feeling from God or the Devil? And if it's God, where's the mercy in that? Forcing me to do that, when He knows how hard it is. Where's His mercy?" I said, inwardly hoping God would hear my lament.

"No. No. You're wrong. God wouldn't make you do that," Zara said, crouching down to my face level and grasping my hands. "God is merciful. He'd never force you to do something He knows you can't do."

So it wasn't God? I wasn't sure who it was then. I knew it couldn't be the Devil, because he'd never want me copying stuff out of God's book.

Even if I wasn't sure who it was, I felt peace knowing now that it wasn't God that was forcing me to copy out verses.

· · ·

"What are you doing?" Adam asked a couple of days later, coming to sit across from me at my mom's dining table.

"Copying verses," I said, rolling up the stacks of paper and sliding on a pink rubber band. "But I'm tired now."

Though I still felt like copying the verses, it wasn't because God was making me feel like I had to. I no longer thought my getting better depended on it. It was something that felt almost cathartic, but now if after even a paragraph I wanted to stop, I just did. I could stop now, without the fear that God would be mad or that I would be doomed to live like this forever. Even the Devil retreated. For some reason, it was like he didn't want to bother with me anymore.

20: MY FRIEND MARILYN

"SO, HOW ARE THINGS WITH YOU NOW?" DR. BAKER asked, swivelling in her office chair to get a good look at me.

"Better, so much better." I noticed for the first time there was a clock positioned carefully by her window, facing both of us. Was it there at our earlier appointments?

"So, are you sleeping better too?" she asked, nodding approvingly.

"Yes, but I get these super vivid espionage-type dreams. They seem so unreal," I said, recalling how the colours and plots of my dreams were wildly fantastical. Every night promised a new action adventure.

"Yes, some people find that happens when they start antidepressants. Are you noticing any other side effects?"

"I don't think so."

"So no urinary hesitancy?"

"What's that?" I asked. The memory of me the night before, on the toilet for two to three hours, hit me. It was so bad that I'd tried to coax it out by running the tap. In the end, I decided it was better to just doze off there and let it come when it wanted to.

"Difficulty urinating," she said. "Antipsychotic medications can be anticholinergic like that at higher doses."

"Oh, okay. I think I have that," I said. "It's a little hard to pee."

"Maybe I should lower your dose."

"No! It's fine, it's not a real problem at all." I didn't want her to lower anything. All I knew was that ever since she'd raised my Seroquels to ten, my life had improved considerably. I didn't know how, but I didn't care. I would go for an entire day without peeing if it meant not going back to the madness of the weeks before.

"I'm so glad you're doing better. We can continue to expect more improvements over the next few weeks as the medications completely hit your system."

The small hand was pointing to the three on the clock. My hour was up.

· · ·

I went to Zara's the next week to visit, but it wasn't like my last trip to her place when I'd needed to increase my Seroquel doses dramatically. It was almost like the old days. We sat together on my old friend, the corduroy sofa, chatting and even laughing about some of the things I'd experienced in the early days of my illness, like my fear of the Angel of Death.

It was obvious I was doing better. The phone rang and Zara went to get it, remaining in the kitchen to answer. She switched to Urdu, and I could tell by the tone of her voice that she was talking to her mom.

Oh, oh, she's gonna tell her mom about you.

I straightened up to peer over at her. Maybe seeing my concerned face would prevent her from talking about me. She nodded and smiled at me, turning her body slightly so I couldn't see her face anymore.

She's telling her mom about you!

Even though Zara's mom was exceptionally nice, I didn't want her to know about my problems. What could I do to make her stop talking about me?

Don't worry, cut off her head so she can't talk anymore!

My eyes grew wide in horror. No, I would never do that. I had the strength to argue back with the thoughts for the first time, ever. I loved Zara. She was my friend.

No problem: put her head on a stake so you can see her forever.
Her decapitated head sat on a stake, reminiscent of the pig's head in Lord of the Flies.

I lay down, revolted.

• • •

Black, gray, and a bit of dusty pink. The colours of my outfit certainly went well together according to the mirror, but was the fact that I'd been insane somehow written on my face, plain as day? I didn't know. I felt like it was, but I was desperate to give Lina the semblance of a normal Eid celebration. I just wanted to go out and be a part of the early-morning festivities at the mosque like everyone else.

"You sure you think I'm okay?" I asked, turning to face Adam.

"Positive," Adam said. "Say the word and we'll leave if you're not," he promised, giving me a hug.

What if you do something crazy? You know, you do take antipsychotics.

The day had gone remarkably well until that thought struck. The dessert plate in my hand trembled. Adam looked up, caught in the middle of giving me a slice of cake. My shallow breathing was enough to convey the message.

"Forget dessert, it's so late. Past Lina's bedtime. Think we'll head out." Was he laying it on a bit thick because we were both already in the dessert line?

I didn't care. I wasn't doing a very good job of looking calm either.

"Thanks, Adam," I said, when we were safely in the car.

"Thank *you*, you were awesome. You lasted all the way until eight o'clock," he said, giving my hand a squeeze.

• • •

"Can I have some more?" I asked, pushing my plate forward. There was only one naan left on the serving plate at my mom's house. Even though I had half in my hand and another on my plate, I felt like I wanted the last remaining one too. The ten pounds that my body had surrendered to the treadmill in those early weeks were aching to get back on my bones. Were carbs always this delicious? I had always been a protein and veggies fan, and breads were something I usually passed on.

I could see my dad eyeing it too. Any other time, I would have readily given it up, but the medications seemed to have opened my eyes to reality, including the reality of delicious food.

"Of course, take it, take it," my dad said, pushing the plate at me. It tilted forward and the naan fell right into the butter chicken on my plate. Yikes, I hated when wet food and dry food mixed. They needed to be kept apart until the right moment.

"Thanks, Dad," I said, trying to salvage the naan by moving it onto the side, away from the chicken. I caught sight of my dad making a swallowing motion, like he was still imagining eating his sacrificed treat.

He was so sweet. I loved him so much. I hoped that I could enjoy his company for many more years.

> *The image of his severed head on a plate, smiling up at me.*

The naan dropped from my hand as disgust and revulsion filled me.

"What happened?" my dad asked.

"Nothing," I said, scrambling to get away from the table. I had been doing so well, and now this! I needed to lie down.

. . .

If only this mall had a Cinnabon, the outing would have been perfect. Nevertheless, I was excited to be able to grab something for Lina. Adam and I held hands, and I marvelled at how different this trip was from the last one. That time I'd been convinced the Devil was trying to talk to me through the music.

"Should we get Lina something from the Disney store?" I asked as I saw it coming up on my right.

"You know that all she loves is books," Adam said.

He was right. Who was I kidding? Maybe it was my own inner kid that wanted a plush stuffie.

A stark, powdery white face. Ultra-black irises surrounded by white pupils, heavily rimmed with teal. Crimson lips, parted widely to reveal sharpened, rotting teeth.

There was the same demonic face that I'd seen, but now it was staring at me from a poster.

"What the hell! Let's go this way," I steered Adam diagonally through the crowds.

"Hey, hey, slow down. Where are you going?" Adam asked.

"I'll tell you after," I said, wanting to make sure we'd made it a safe distance away. "But look at the poster outside the HMV store."

"The one of Marylin Manson?"

"You *know* him?" I asked, unable to hide my shock.

"Who doesn't? That guy took Marylin Monroe's first name and Charles Manson's last name and made it his. Quite ingenious." Adam was giving me a history lesson on musical icons, like he always did. My lack of musical awareness was finally coming to bite me in the butt. I didn't want to tell him that the Devil I'd seen before looked an awful lot like Marylin Manson; indeed, was easily his twin.

"I just don't like his face," I said, shuddering. "It's scary."

• • •

"Can you hurry?" I asked, my anxiety reaching a crescendo.

"What do you want me to do, speed?" Adam asked. I did and I didn't. But even if he did speed, there were just too many cars piled nose to tail. I didn't want to miss my appointment with Dr. Baker. I really looked forward to the weekly one-hour sessions.

Why did Adam always have to wait until the last minute to start the forty-five-minute trek downtown? Maybe he liked the thrill of driving like he was in a NASCAR race. Yes, that was it. I recalled that the drive to deliver Lina had been like this too, chaotic and fast, every bump painful to my waiting-to-burst belly.

"We could've left earlier," I said, snapping. He was acting like it wasn't his fault.

"So what are you suggesting I do?" he snapped back, trying to weave around the surrounding cars, who seemed to delight in being at a standstill.

Honks. The cars apparently weren't as happy as they seemed.

"Do you want to get out and walk or something? It's not that far," he offered. Not that far? I wasn't capable of flying. Even if we were only three minutes away by car, it would take me at least half an hour to walk there, and at that point, who knows? My appointment slot would likely be swallowed up by some other needy woman. My breathing was coming fast.

"Just tell me what's going to help," Adam said.

Just drink the bottle of Febreze.

Just drink the bottle of Febreze? Did that thought actually cross my mind? I looked down at the Febreze bottle at my feet. I kept it in the car for emergencies, because my mother was always cooking potent, delicious curries that were a joy to eat but not to wear. *Just drink the bottle of Febreze.* It was a bizarre, strange thought. I definitely needed to get to today's appointment.

I tumbled out of the car thirty seconds from my destination and ran like the Devil was behind me.

"Aaisha! I was wondering where you were. You're always on time," Dr. Baker said as I came stumbling into the waiting area.

"Sorry, I was running late," I said, trying to catch my breath. We walked together down the hallway, and I noticed that her long legs were no longer hard to keep up with.

"So, tell me, how are you doing?" she asked, settling into her chair. The clock told me I'd already missed twenty minutes of my hour. She caught me looking at it and shook her head like I shouldn't bother about it, but it did bother me.

"I'm so much better," I said, being conscious of the list I needed to get through. "But I can still see that I'm not fully better. Like sometimes when I get stressed, weird things pop into my head," I said, thinking about the idea of drinking Febreze.

"Give me an example," she said.

"Well, like one time I was stressed about something, and it popped into my head that maybe I should just drink a bottle of Febreze," I said, feeling stupid.

"Hm." I wondered if she was contemplating calling some men in white to take me away.

"How did you feel about that?" she asked.

"Well, I knew it was crazy and made no sense."

She nodded.

"Aaisha, you have to understand that you have been very sick. It seems like whenever the stress is too much, you crack a little."

I pictured a delicate hairline crack on my head, like what I sometimes saw on eggs when I pulled them from the carton and examined them closely.

"So that's normal?" I asked, wondering if I'd always be a damaged egg.

"For now. You're still fragile. It's only been a month since I started seeing you. Take it easy, and maybe we can talk about some techniques to relieve stress next time." I left, imagining an egg with its top wrapped in bandages like it'd just had a lobotomy.

• • •

I will always be incredibly grateful to Dr. Baker for the amount of time she allotted to my appointments.

It is often acknowledged that women from different backgrounds describe symptoms of postpartum mood disorders in different ways. This is why healthcare providers are encouraged to develop cultural competency and provide culturally sensitive and appropriate care. Cultural competency is without a doubt very important. What I don't believe is discussed enough is that these alternative ways of explaining symptoms may also require the investment of more time on the part of healthcare providers.

With more and more psychiatrists limiting themselves to simply doing fifteen-minute medication check-ins, spending time with patients experiencing mental-health issues is becoming a dying art form.[1] And lack of time with patients is dangerous. It can contribute to tragedies like that of Andrea Yates drowning her five children. According to *Are You There Alone?: The Unspeakable Crime of Andrea Yates*, a book by Suzanne O'Malley, the nursing staff at Devereux Texas Treatment Network in League City, Texas, reported that they only saw Yates's psychiatrist visiting her for a combined total of a single hour during the twenty-four days she was an inpatient prior to the drownings.[2] I can't help but wonder if what befell Andrea would have happened at all had she received the investment of time and care I did with Dr. Baker.

What would help every woman with a postpartum mood disorder is having a provider who takes the time to really listen and understand what is going on, even if it takes more than fifteen minutes.

21: IS THIS YOUR WIFE?

MY SYMPTOMS WERE SLOWLY REVERSING IN THE SAME order as they had first appeared. First, the new dimension I had merged with disappeared, and then the battle between God and the Devil suddenly ceased to exist. Soon after, the violent commands, thoughts, and images dissipated, then even the bizarre thoughts left me. But I was still far from my baseline.

"I feel like I'm such a loser!" I said, slumping into my chair in Dr. Baker's office. I no longer needed her to escort me down the long corridor. Ms. Reproductive-Mental-Health at the front desk would just tell me Dr. Baker was ready for me, and I would go by myself.

"What do you mean?" Dr. Baker asked, leaning forward to meet my gaze.

"I can't seem to do anything. I can't even offer to read a picture book to Lina because my concentration is shot," I said. "Sometimes I am even scared of Lina," I said.

"What do you mean?" she asked, sitting up with her lips pursed, eyes narrowed.

"Well, I feel like she's smarter than me, the way she's able to read all these chapter books," I said.

"Wait. Lina, your five-year-old daughter, can read chapter books?" Dr. Baker asked, looking incredulous.

"Yes, well she started reading chapter books when she was still three," I said, feeling entirely the opposite of a proud mother.

"Your daughter, she's a genius!" Dr. Baker exclaimed.

"But I'm such a loser, and she's so much smarter than me!" I moaned.

"Look, Aaisha, I told you that you were really, really sick, and you needed to cut yourself some slack. You've already come so far in so little time."

She was sweet to try to make me feel less down on myself. Obviously, it was never okay to tell a patient that they were, by all standards, a loser.

"I want you to do something. I want you to start journaling, so that you can see just how much more you are able to do each day."

I wasn't sure how that would help me, but I loved this woman for her valiant efforts.

Nov. 6, 2006
"I am grateful to be able to close my eyes and just see darkness and feel serene."

"I am grateful to be able to urinate without difficulty or too much hesitation."

"I am grateful to be able to sleep."

Nov. 7, 2006
"I am grateful to be able to do housework."

Nov. 10, 2006
"I am grateful for feeling like taking my daughter places."

Nov. 11, 2006
"I am grateful to have had a whole day of feeling

well and worrying about normal things, like how Adam doesn't have a job."

Nov. 13, 2006
"I am grateful to be able to read books."

. . .

"So you're *sure* I didn't get sick because of my house?" I asked for the fourth time.

"Yes. You had postpartum depression with psychotic features, also known as postpartum psychosis. It had nothing to do with your house," Dr. Baker said. Was that a hint of exasperation I was hearing?

"But how come whenever I'm even near my house, I get this knot in my chest, and it gets really hard for me to breathe? It's almost exactly how I felt when I started getting sick." I could have sworn that my house was possessed, if I believed in such things.

"Your illness was so traumatizing that I think you've associated it negatively with your house," she said.

It made sense to me that the mind could make connections between disparate events, but this didn't feel like a merely tangential association. It felt visceral.

"So, you're absolutely sure that just being in my house won't make me sick again?" I wished she could give me a signed and sealed guarantee, one that I could thrust at the thoughts and feelings to make them crawl back to the hole they'd come from.

"Look, when you are ready, you'll be able to go back home, and you won't even need to give it a second thought. For now, just go for short visits. Take a Seroquel to calm yourself when you do go."

. . .

Nov. 25, 2006
"I am grateful to have a second chance at life!"

Two months to the day I left there, I was finally back at home.

"Remember when Idris started dancing like a robot?" Zara asked, hardly able to control her laughter. The image of my brother dancing like a robot filled my mind.

"That was craz—," I stopped, right in the middle of fluffing my pillows. Who was I talking to? I was alone in my bedroom, but I'd heard Zara's voice as clearly as if she was standing right next to me.

Did everyone hear the voices of loved ones in their head as they were getting ready for bed? I wanted to ask Adam, but he was out running an errand. I could call and ask Zara.

"Hey, Zara. Quick question. Do you ever hear voices of friends or family when you are getting ready for bed?"

"Huh? What do you mean Aaisha?"

"Like do you hear voices, like your mom's or sister's in your head when —" Hearing myself say it out loud dispelled my confusion. "Sorry, I think I'm really tired, I better let you go to sleep, and I'll go to sleep myself," I said, embarrassed.

"Okay, bye," Zara said.

Dr. Baker had told me I could try to lower my night-time dose of Seroquel that day. It was something Adam and I had celebrated with a Cinnabon. But maybe it was still a little too early for that. I swallowed another pill before hopping into bed.

• • •

Dec. 12, 2006
"I am grateful for being able to fall asleep on one quarter of a Seroquel."

Dec. 14, 2006

"I am grateful that I slept last night with no Seroquel."

. . .

Adam settled into his seat beside me. I could see him looking around uncomfortably. He'd stopped coming to every single session since I started improving, but Dr. Baker had specially requested that he attend this one.

"Well, thanks for coming in," she said to Adam, giving him a warm smile.

He nodded.

"I wanted to ask you something."

We were all ears.

"Is this your wife?"

I looked at her, astounded. What kind of question was that?

"What I mean is, this Aaisha talks a lot, is animated, and full of energy. Is this her 'normal'?"

Adam broke into a wide grin. "Yes, this is normal, who Aaisha was before she got sick."

I couldn't contain my own smile.

"But this Aaisha is so different from the one I first met. *Very* different," she said, unable to hide her shock.

"Yes, but this is the Aaisha I married and have always known," Adam confirmed.

I had been saying the same to Dr. Baker ever since glimmers of the old me started coming back. She had been constantly checking that the animated, conversational version of me was part of my baseline and not a sign of mania or hypomania. I felt vindicated.

• • •

It was mid-December, two and half months since I had been correctly diagnosed, and I was finally completely off the Seroquel. I had been told that I would need to remain on the Effexor for at least another year. Which was fine by me.

The initial elation of getting my life back was soon replaced with anger and resentment. I couldn't get over the feeling that my family had failed me, Adam had failed me even more, and that because of their ignorance, Lina and I could have ended up dead, or I could have ended up institutionalized for the rest of my life.

Though the couples therapy that Dr. Baker recommended was supposed to help me deal with my resentment, it did little to resolve it. And the lavish dinners Adam treated me to after each session did nothing but help me gain back the weight I lost.

Then, out of the blue. Nadia happened.

• • •

> Dec. 22, 2006
> "I am grateful that Nadia, Omar, and the baby are alive."
>
> Dec. 23, 2006
> "I am grateful …"

I couldn't finish the entry. I was simultaneously livid and sad about what I had learned from attending Nadia's first meeting with the hospital psychiatrist after being admitted. It turned out that she had actually gone to her family doctor earlier that day, just before my parents and I arrived for the intervention.

She had told him how miserable she was and that she wanted to get away from her kids. Despite this, he didn't ask her any further questions or even do a depression inventory on her. Instead, he sent her home, telling her she'd soon be better.

I couldn't believe that had it not been for me, who was still in the early weeks of recovering from postpartum psychosis myself, she and her kids could have ended up dead. And society would have acted like there was nothing that could have been done to prevent the tragedy.

It was close to midnight when, with my gratitude journal still open in my hand, I started bawling. I had tried to keep the sadness from welling up in me for as long as I could. So, when the dam broke, torrents of tears poured out.

"What's wrong?" Adam said, coming up to me as I sat on the bed, heaving uncontrollably.

"Nadia and her kids could have died," I said haltingly, almost unable to get the words out.

"But they didn't," he said, kneeling next to me. "Thanks to you."

"Don't you get it? That's exactly the problem."

"You're not making any sense," he said, getting to his feet. "Do you need to take a Seroquel?"

I wasn't psychotic. What was he talking about?

"Don't you get it? The world is *crazy* if you have to rely on one insane person to get help for another insane person. Why are all the sane people of the world just sitting around, not helping?"

"You're getting sick. Is it too late to call Dr. Baker?"

"I'm not sick! I'm just sick and tired of people suffering and dying because of this illness while sane people are ignorant."

"If you don't take that Seroquel right now, I'm calling the police."

Thump, thump, thump. Ten minutes later, the police were at our door. I heard Adam speaking in muffled tones.

Two cops came into my room. Muscular and chiseled, they had guns secured in holsters. For the second time in less than a week, I was closer to guns than I had ever been in my whole life.

I had been rehearsing what I was going to say since I'd heard Adam place the call. I had wanted to yell at him, but I knew that would feed even more into his notion that I was losing it.

"So, what's going on, ma'am?" asked one of them, whose badge read "Todd."

"Nothing," I said. "Well, my husband thinks I'm psychotic."

Two pairs of eyes looked at me, encouraging me to continue.

"I had postpartum psychosis a while ago," I said. "I'm cured now, and off my antipsychotic medication. A few days ago, a woman I know was experiencing many of the same symptoms I'd had. She was psychotic and felt like killing her son. I knew she was sick and intervened to get her to the hospital."

They looked from me to each other like they thought I was the one who was crazy.

I gulped. "You can call your department to confirm what I just told you. You'll see, the police had to come to escort us to the hospital."

That seemed to convince them I knew what I was talking about.

"So why does your husband think you're psychotic now?" Todd asked.

"Because I was crying and upset. But I'm upset because I just found out that the sick woman's doctor had sent her home the same day I intervened. He didn't help her, and that put her and her whole family at risk. That's why I was upset, because even doctors are so ignorant of this condition." I looked up, unsure if I made any sense.

"Look, if you want me to take my antipsychotic medication I will, or if you want me to go get checked out at the hospital, I'll go with you."

They looked at each other, and even though no words were exchanged between them, Todd spoke for both. "We think you're fine. But do either of you have somewhere else to spend the night?"

I nodded, unsure why they were asking this. "We suggest you spend the night away from each other, so you can both calm down."

They left. I dialed Zara. No need to unnecessarily worry my parents.

• • •

I honestly can't blame Adam for getting nervous and calling the police on me when he thought I was psychotic again and refusing to take medication. He had twice been witness to how badly things can go wrong when a serious issue is treated with indifference. However, because of his own worry about my mental health, he wasn't processing that I had good reason to weep.

Despite having been raised as a fierce advocate for things I am passionate about, it was incredibly difficult for me to find help. This was partly because of the ignorance that shrouds this illness, but also because I am a woman of colour. The difficulties experienced by women of colour who have postpartum mood disorders is only amplified when it comes to immigrant women of colour like Nadia. It is widely acknowledged that immigrants face higher rates of postpartum mood disorders than non-immigrant women.[1] This has been linked to a number of factors, including isolation and the lack of social support many experience due to being new to a country.

Difficulties in getting help are also compounded because of communication barriers. In my own work, I have experienced the difficulty of trying to connect women who speak little English to community resources.

Translation services can be useful in some circumstances, but are not as helpful in cases where a woman is experiencing a disorder like postpartum psychosis. The clinical diagnosis of postpartum psychosis relies heavily on a detailed case history and a thorough description of symptoms.[2] Unlike with severe physical illnesses, there are no objective tests like CT scans or MRIs that can help paint a picture of what is wrong and confirm or deny the presence of delusions or hallucinations.

Additionally, the symptoms of postpartum psychosis often include paranoia and severe distrust, sometimes even of family, healthcare providers, and anyone else trying to help. This paranoia was why Nadia was accusing me of lying and being evil when I showed up at her house to help her.

Even when I was able to gain Nadia's trust, and though her command of English was fairly strong, there were times when I ran into trouble with trying to help her. On several occasions while she was at the hospital, I had to enlist the help of my husband to translate some of what she was experiencing. This was because she was only able to describe some of these complicated experiences in her native language of Pashto, which, fortunately, Adam spoke and understood.

North America has some of the best healthcare resources in the world, and it is imperative that we ensure that these resources are used to help everyone, regardless of their background.

22: WAS I LIKE THIS?

"VISITING TIME IS OVER," THE NURSE WITH THE pinched face announced, popping her head into Nadia's room a couple of days later. I was happy to see the nurse, even though she was one of the mean ones.

I got up slowly from my gray industrial chair. Every time I came, I had to haul it from the hallway into the room, because this was the kind of room that couldn't have anything extra in it. It wasn't really a mystery why.

When Nadia was admitted, the floor had been quiet because it was two thirty in the morning. During normal waking hours, it was anything but that. Screams, gut-wrenching wails, and screeches capable of penetrating walls often filled the hallways.

My parents had expressed the desire to visit Nadia themselves, but after my first morning visit, I'd advised them not to come. I was afraid they would be frightened. Not long ago, I too might have interpreted such sounds as scary, and the people making them as frightening. But my own illness allowed me to perceive the sounds in an entirely new light. To me now, they were the attempts to cope by people who, not unlike me when I was sick, were extremely frightened by what was happening to them.

As I bent over to give Nadia a goodbye hug, I couldn't help but feel secretly happy that it was the end of visiting hours. It was exhausting to deal with Nadia's ups and downs. She vacillated back and forth, sometimes grateful to me for bringing her to the hospital, sometimes hating me for complicating her life.

The only consistent thing was the forlorn look she would give me when visiting hours were over. Luckily, I knew just what to say to turn her frown upside down.

"I'll be back tomorrow," I said. She smiled up at me weakly.

• • •

I'd desperately wanted to be at the hospital when I was ill. Without a doubt, it is the best place for a woman experiencing the more acute and dangerous symptoms of postpartum psychosis. However, North America has a long way to go in terms of getting care for mothers with severe mental illness right. In many parts of the world, there are actually inpatient mother and baby psychiatric units. In these units, moms, babies, and in some cases even partners, are allowed to be together.[1] Countries that have these programs include Australia, Belgium, France, India, the Netherlands, New Zealand, and the U.K.[2]

Good care programs such as these recognize all the essentials when it comes to postpartum psychosis. Namely, that a mom with this condition is *not* a bad mom but *is* suffering from a severe illness. She is not safe to make decisions for herself or her baby at the moment, but she *can* get better and go on to care for her infant. And lastly, a mother suffering from postpartum psychosis is still worthy and deserving of being near to and surrounded by her loved ones.

• • •

"I can't believe you're well enough to be able to leave the hospital," I said about two weeks later. After a little more than a week on heavy antipsychotics, Nadia's psychiatrist had deemed her stable enough for outside visits of up to three hours. However, this permission came with the promise that she would be supervised the entire time, never left alone, and be dropped back at the hospital by 8:00 p.m.

Worry cast a shadow over Nadia's face. "But I don't want to go home. I think my house is haunted," she said.

"It's not haunted," I said, trying to get her out of her hospital slippers into her boots. All of Nadia's things were stuffed into a big plastic bag, which the nurse with the pinched face had handed me when I'd arrived to pick Nadia up. For some reason, it always seemed like it was this nurse who was on duty whenever I came to visit.

"You're scared of your house because that's where you got sick. I felt like that too. Trust me, it's not haunted."

"But yesterday, when Mikhail took me home and I went to the bathroom," she paused, "I saw the Devil's face in the mirror where my face should have been," she said in a sharp whisper. Her eyebrows were raised, mimicking the pure fright she had felt when she saw it.

I nodded, remembering the makeup session that I thought had been hijacked by the Devil. The similarities in symptoms between our illnesses were eerie.

"I know. Mikhail told me," I said, tugging out her jacket from the gigantic plastic bag that held the elements of her former life. "But you'll be fine today. We aren't taking you home."

I looped my arm through hers like we were old school-chums. "You're coming to my mom's with me!" I said, leading the way out of Nadia's hospital room.

"She has to be back by eight, and she's not to be left alone — ever," the sour-looking nurse barked as we stood at the

Plexiglass-lined nursing station. We waited patiently for permission to pass through the alarmed doors.

I nodded eagerly, internally wanting to please her. I got the sense she didn't like me or trust me. I couldn't figure out which. Or maybe it was just that she wasn't used to seeing many visitors for those on this ward. Whatever it was, she made me want to leave even faster than I was already ready to.

. . .

The heavy scent of basmati rice intertwined with spices that came wafting as we opened the door nearly spoiled the surprise. My mom's shy smile awaited us at the entry. I noticed she was wearing the peacock-printed apron that I'd gifted her a few Eids back. There was a deep crimson stain across the chest, right over the peacock's magnificent tail. As usual, the apron hung in front of her like a shield, its strings untied.

She embraced Nadia warmly, leaning into the hug an additional two times. It was the traditional Muslim hug, the type shared between family and friends on happy occasions like Eid. The hug made sense, since Nadia's return to sanity was truly something to celebrate.

"Welcome," my dad called, descending the stairs from his office. The smiles on all our faces made a vast contrast to the last time we gathered together.

My mom's huge dining table was set for four, but the spread on it didn't look like it was just for four. Fresh garden salad, naan, spiced yogurt, and an eggplant dish that I knew took hours to make were arrayed on the slatted bamboo table-runner. And then came the pièce de résistance: lamb biryani. It was something I knew my mom had gone to great lengths to make for Nadia. We'd figured she'd be sick of hospital food and would relish having a good home-cooked Indo-Pak meal. How my sixty-year-old mother could pull that off while simultaneously helping to care for Nadia's kids was a mystery to me.

I scanned the table, watching happily as Nadia positioned herself across from my mother and me. My mom, as was typical for her, spent most of the time bustling back and forth from the kitchen, topping up dishes and getting drinks. Nadia nibbled on the lamb biryani, but I noticed she was picking at her food, not even pretending to like it.

Even though I knew intimately what Nadia was going through, and that she was still ill, I couldn't help but feel irritation rise up inside of me. It was like she didn't seem to *notice* all the trouble my parents and even Zara were going through for her: cooking for her, taking turns caring for her kids, and supporting her. She was consistently elsewhere, somewhere, lost in her head.

Was this what I was like when I was sick?

Guilt pulsed through me as I thought of Mariya's quivering lip as she tried to feed me soup when I was ill and the look on her face when I punched her for trying to stop me from running after Adam. I recalled my mom's haggard eyes during those dark nights as she hugged me tight, muttering prayers while she stroked my hair.

"Can I talk to you alone?" Nadia asked abruptly.

"Sure," I said. I led her down the creaky stairs to my parents' packed basement. We sat together on the faded peach sofa.

"This is all Mikhail's fault," she said, grabbing one of the colourful throw pillows and squeezing it tightly in front of her chest. She didn't seem lost in thought now, more so overly focused. Her eyes were narrowed and her eyebrows heavily knitted together.

I blinked at her, wanting to figure out what she was talking about. Everything I had seen of Mikhail over the past two weeks suggested he was an angel of a husband. He never raised his voice in anger or frustration and was constantly massaging Nadia's back, legs, or arms and murmuring quiet things into her ears while she scowled or blurted out angry orders at him. Maybe my assessment of him had been wrong?

"I'm sick because he didn't do what he was supposed to do," she said. "I need him to tell off his sister back home. It's because she doesn't like me that this happened. But he's not telling her off. Can you talk to him?" she asked. She had a pleading look in her eyes. "If he just did that from the beginning, I would never have gotten sick. It's all *her* fault …"

As I sat listening to Nadia ramble on about her delusion, I remembered how I'd sat on this very sofa, blaming Adam for my woes. *If Adam would just have reminded me that I wasn't going crazy and countered my thoughts, I wouldn't have gotten sick*, is what I had thought at the time. As though thinking positive thoughts could have cured psychosis. I recalled the fury I'd experienced whenever he mentioned taking medication.

And as I continued listening to Nadia, something began to dawn on me. What must it have felt like to be Adam, to watch the woman you love unravel before your eyes while the doctors you took her to did nothing to help? For the first time since I'd gotten sick, I realized that the horror of my illness was not mine alone. My illness had been horrifying to my loved ones as well. Not only horrifying, but likely also extremely confusing.

That evening, after dropping Nadia back at the hospital, I crawled into bed beside Adam. In the darkness, I lay my head on his chest and wrapped my arm around him, like I used to before postpartum psychosis struck. "You know, I never asked you how you felt when I got sick," I said.

I could feel the familiar rhythmic beating coming from his chest while I waited for his answer.

"I was scared that I was losing you and that I would never get you back," he said, wrapping his own arm around me.

• • •

"We better hurry if we wanna catch them," Adam said.

"Departures are this way," I said, pointing to the sign. We raced, but Adam's strides were longer, even if mine were faster. The sterile silver gates were surrounded by crops of people with luggage huddled together. Animated talk and laughter erupted from these groups, punctuated by the occasional announcement of a flight delay blaring harshly over the speakers.

"Aaisha, you made it!" Nadia said, smiling widely and enveloping me in a hug. We'd basically been complete strangers when we first met, but being her sole visitor while she was in the mental-health ward for three weeks had earned me her affection.

"You're leaving," I said, clasping both her hands.

"Yes, but I'm not sure if I can do it, or even if I should," she said, anxiety clouding her face momentarily.

"It'll be good for you. Remember, your doctor said the support will be helpful. You can do it. In no time at all, you'll be back home visiting your mom and wondering why you ever doubted going," I said.

"We have to get to the gate," Mikhail said, coming over.

I nodded. "Do you have my phone number?"

"Yes," Nadia said, tapping her head.

"Write it down before you forget!" I said, pulling out an old receipt to scrawl my number on.

"No way. I'll never forget you or your number, not after everything you did for me. You've been a good friend. You've been my friend, a mother, and a sister to me during all of this."

"Don't forget to send me your new number when you get there," I said, leaning in to give her a hug. My eyes didn't care that I'd promised not to cry.

EXPLANATORY NOTES ON MY SECOND DESCENT INTO MADNESS

After my miscarriage, the sadness I experienced was labelled simply "grief" by my doctor. The thing is, I didn't feel like I was grieving my miscarriage anymore, but I was still experiencing sadness that was concerning. This should have inspired my doctor to at least do a depression inventory on me. As my postpartum psychosis escalated, I was not able to accurately label what was happening to me. But now, I have more clarity about some of the things I was going through then.

The stressful, repetitive thoughts urging me to get organized were called "ruminations" by my doctor. A rumination is when someone thinks the same thoughts over and over again. "Auditory hallucinations" are sounds or voices in the absence of auditory stimuli; they can be perceived as either internal or external, meaning they can be heard as being inside one's head or as coming from outside. I am pretty sure that my repeating thoughts took on qualities of auditory hallucinations when they became loud and started saying distressing things to me. When I heard the Devil speaking to me at the mall, and later believed that he was telling me to swear at God, those were very obvious instances of auditory hallucinations coming from outside my head.

The fact that I did not perceive the loud thoughts as my own was also a troubling sign. Pretty early on, I became convinced my thoughts were not mine but were coming from somewhere else. Later, I came to believe the thoughts were put there by the Devil and, in one case, even by God. This is an example of a delusional belief called "thought insertion." Thought insertion is when an individual believes their thoughts are not their own and have been put into their head by someone or something else. Unfortunately, this was something I kept to myself for too long, believing it was a religious experience that those not of my faith wouldn't be able to understand.

At least one of the auditory hallucinations I experienced also had a component called "delusion of reference." A delusion of reference is when an individual perceives random events as referring to them directly or having special significance. The hallucination I experienced at the mall, in which I heard violent words in the music, is an example of a delusion of reference. In my mind, the music was specifically a medium for the Devil to communicate with me.

The auditory hallucination involving the Devil ordering me to swear at God was also a very specific kind of hallucination called a "command hallucination." The voice was ordering me to do something in a very menacing manner, making me feel I had no choice but to obey. This particular symptom was extremely frightening, as its threatening nature took away my sense of control.

Another type of delusion I experienced in this bout of postpartum psychosis was a "delusion of influence." This type of delusion involves a person falsely believing something or someone other than themself is influencing their thoughts or actions. This was by far one of the most terrifying experiences that I went through. Delusions of influence were manifested for me when I believed the Devil was controlling me, urging me to shove people onto the street and to throw myself into traffic. These were overwhelming urges that I felt forced to comply with. They felt entirely outside of my control and completely opposed to what I really wanted to do.

Both command hallucinations and delusions of influence feel like they strip you of your ability to choose for yourself and exert control over yourself. I didn't *want* to hurt myself or anyone else. This was made clear by everything I did to stop myself from giving in to the urges, including crying, praying, crossing the street, gripping my husband's hand, and lastly, begging to be locked up.

As for the things I saw at this time, I think initially they *may* have been intrusive thoughts. I say this because early on, at some level, I knew they were a product of my mind. I didn't think they really existed for real in the outside world and, in at least one case, I was in a position to question the reality of what I saw. However, this is not to say that the thoughts weren't extremely distressing and frightening in their own right.

Later on, however, I started to experience full-blown visual hallucinations that seemed completely real. I couldn't recognize them as being a product of my mind at all. Some of these visual hallucinations included the corpses I saw hanging from Zara's ceiling, the ghostly white trees that I believed the Devil would hang corpses on, and the walls morphing. There was absolutely no way anyone could have convinced me they were a product of my mind. This is because to me they were as real as my own hands. Even after I fully recovered, I couldn't get over how real they'd been to me, and I kept asking Dr. Baker how they could have felt so real if they weren't.

My hope is that this section clarifies the difference between the psychotic elements of my illness compared to the depressive and anxiety-related ones. As I'm sure is clear, my second experience with postpartum psychosis was much worse than my first. I can't help but wonder if this could have been mitigated if I'd received treatment the first time. However, even the second time, I'm sure I would have benefited much faster if the doctors I went to were better informed of this illness and had diagnosed it at the onset of my symptoms.

Regardless, I am grateful that the psychiatrist I went to saw immediately how ill I was. To me, this shows the importance of having your symptoms checked out by a psychiatrist if you or a loved one experiences concerning psychiatric symptoms in the postpartum period. This should be the case even when you have no previous psychiatric history, but especially if you do.

The last thing I want is for people to read this book and immediately think they have postpartum psychosis. If you suspect you have it, or someone you know has it, don't hesitate to advocate for help. There is help available, and there are organizations out there dedicated to helping you find it. Developing postpartum psychosis does not need to be the end of the world.

• • •

Given the religious delusions I experienced during my second time with postpartum psychosis, some may wonder what I truly believe about the role religion and God played in my illness. When Dr. Baker learned of the true extent of my religious delusions as I got better, she was floored. She asked how it was that I managed to come in and continue seeing her, despite feeling like I couldn't reveal everything to her because she wasn't Muslim.

I didn't know then what to say, but I do now. My religious delusions may have prevented me from getting proper help sooner, but God is why I was sent Dr. Baker and Seroquel.

EPILOGUE

NEARLY A YEAR AFTER MY SECOND FORAY INTO POST-partum psychosis, I still found it mesmerizing to experience silence in my head and just see pure blackness as I lay in bed with my eyes closed.

The phone rang, forcing me to whip my eyes open to answer it.

"Yes, that day and time works perfectly for me," I said.

I was eager to participate in the opportunity Dr. Baker had recommended me for. The strides I had made in my own healing, and the way that helping Nadia had resolved my own resentment toward my family, had given Dr. Baker an idea.

"It seems like helping others with this illness really is helpful to your own healing," she had remarked.

It was true. The illness seemed less bleak when I felt I was active-ly doing something to help someone else avoid suffering like I did.

"You know, I think you would be an excellent person to partici-pate in medical education. You could share your story with second-year medical students in a role we call a teaching patient. As you saw, the medical education of doctors is woefully lacking when it comes to mental illness. It would help them learn to avoid the same mistakes you experienced."

One of the biggest horrors of my illness was the experience of being turned away by the healthcare professionals I went to for help.

And here I was being given the opportunity to change that! If even a handful of future doctors heard my story and learned from it not to turn away a new mom in distress, or if it made them realize the importance of doing a depression inventory on someone, my contribution would be monumental.

And so, less than a year after my own recovery, I began volunteering as a teaching patient with the hospital's Medical Education Department. As a teaching patient, I helped future doctors learn about the symptoms of this illness as they practiced their psychiatric interviewing skills.

Shortly after that, I decided to volunteer with various maternal mental-health organizations. Despite going back to my day job, my mission after hours was to make sure no woman fell through the cracks in her or her family's bid to get help and support. If someone or their loved one was experiencing the symptoms of postpartum psychosis, I wanted to help make sure they got the right type of help.

As the years since my recovery passed, I came to learn many things that I'd never realized or understood while I was ill. For one, I learned that when all the doctors had initially turned me away, it had made many people in my family wonder if I was simply seeking attention or being a hypochondriac. In their minds, if something were truly wrong with me other than the grief from my miscarriage, at least *one* of the five healthcare providers I sought out would have said as much. I bear no malice toward anyone in my family who thought this. In fact, I can't say that I wouldn't have thought the same. The blame for this fully lies with the healthcare professionals who were ignorant about this illness and may have been acting on their own biases, consciously or unconsciously.

The only person who never doubted that something was seriously wrong with me was Adam. However, he felt overwhelmed and powerless to do anything in the face of the doctors who believed I was coping well and doing fine.

I hadn't been able to recognize all those who stepped in to care for Lina while I was so sick, lost in my own world. Adam, my parents, and Mariya were instrumental in giving Lina the support and love she needed. In fact, Adam's extended leave from work to take care of Lina and me ended up costing him his job for a second time. I am eternally grateful for him making the sacrifice to be there for us both times. Lina being just fine, in spite of all that happened, is in so many ways attributable to my family being there for her.

It is truly not easy to care for someone with a severe mental illness. I will always be grateful for the support I got from Mariya and Zara during that difficult time in my life. As for my parents, they have both become mental-health crusaders. Just as they'd done with Nadia, if they notice people in our local community suffering from what appears to be depression or anxiety, they are quick to befriend them, try to destigmatize their mental-health struggles, and connect them to me.

Nadia has continued to stay in touch with me for well over a decade. I get at least twice-yearly reports on how she is doing and how her children are growing up. Unlike those early days when it seemed she wasn't as grateful as she could have been, she is always eager to ask about my parents and Zara. She is always quick to recollect that they were there for her in the most difficult period of her life and asks me to pass her good wishes along to them.

As for where I am today, I am completely healed from having had postpartum psychosis and have never experienced any symptoms since. With proper treatment, this is truly a temporary illness. If you met me today, you'd never know that I had ever experienced postpartum psychosis. Adam has continued to be a pillar of strength and support for me and is never reluctant to pat himself on the back for being the only one that recognized how sick I was. And Lina today is a brilliant, beautiful young lady. She is none the worse for having lost four months of her infancy and several months of her early childhood to my illness. Children are remarkably resilient, especially when they have the love and support of others, like Lina did. What is most important is that she knows that with the right kind of education and help, this illness is easily treatable and doesn't need to be a secret.

AFTERWORD

IF SOMEONE HAD TOLD ME TWENTY YEARS AGO THAT I would someday be diagnosed with a condition described in the bible of mental illnesses, *The Diagnostic and Statistical Manual for Mental Disorders* (DSM), I would have laughed. If they told me that the illness would render me insane, I would never have believed it.

Having done my undergraduate thesis in psychology with a professor whose research interest lay in psychotic disorders, it was inevitable that I would end up knowing at least something about the topic. Off the top of my head, I knew the distinguishing features of illnesses classified as psychoses. This list includes two particularly frightening symptoms: delusions and hallucinations. Simply stated, illnesses that fit this category involve individuals losing touch with reality, or what is colloquially called "losing your mind."

"Postpartum psychosis" (PPP) is a psychiatric emergency. It strikes as many as one to two out of every thousand women who deliver a baby.[1] When that one out of a thousand happens to be you, a loved one, or someone you know, its relatively low incidence means little. It should mean even less when you consider that women afflicted with PPP have a 10 percent suicide/infanticide rate.[2] PPP has been at the root of too many tragedies involving a new mother taking her own life or that of her child or children.

Although PPP shares some of its symptoms with other types of psychoses, it is also unique. Postpartum psychosis is, as its name suggests, a condition that can only afflict women who are postpartum. More clearly stated, it afflicts those who were pregnant. The pregnancy need not have resulted in a baby, but may have resulted in a miscarriage, still birth, or termination.

People often confuse postpartum psychosis with conditions like postpartum depression and the baby blues. "Postpartum depression" (PPD) is a more common, and, thankfully, less serious condition that afflicts 21 percent of new moms.[3] "Baby blues," experienced by 60–80 percent of new mothers,[4] is not an illness and is a normal period of adjustment, unlike PPD or PPP. Both PPD and PPP, and indeed all the other postpartum mood disorders, have specific criteria for diagnosis, while the baby blues does not.

No one knows for sure why PPP afflicts only some women. Risk factors have been identified. But the risk factors are just that, risk *factors*. They are not the only factors that can cause someone to fall prey to this illness — a fact I quickly learned.

Experts suspect that PPP has a biological component[5] or has to do with a severe reaction to the changes in pregnancy hormones triggered by delivering a baby, with some women being more sensitive than others. Even more puzzling is that women who have experienced PPP with one pregnancy may not necessarily experience it with another. Nevertheless, chances of illness do increase with every pregnancy following one with PPP or PPD.

A diagnosis of PPP necessitates the presence of at least one of the following criteria: delusions or hallucinations. Other characteristics of this condition include paranoia, severe agitation, insomnia, bizarre violent thoughts, and disorganized thought, behaviour, and speech.

Looking at the two main symptoms of PPP, one may think they appear clear enough. In fact, having studied them in detail in my undergraduate years, I was convinced that they were pretty straight-forward. But nothing could be further from the truth. "Delusions" are generally defined as false beliefs that persist despite evidence to the contrary. It is easy to know if something is a false belief when you are not psychotic. However, as my experience showed, when you are psychotic you don't know that what you are thinking is false. The belief makes total sense to you (e.g., I believed my scary thoughts were coming from the Devil), which is why you believe it in the first place.

What further exacerbates the situation is if the false belief or paranoia involves your support structure, or worse, your healthcare provider (e.g., I wouldn't tell Dr. Baker about the Devil, because she wasn't Muslim). When this happens, any attempt to convince you of anything, including the fact that you are ill or that what you are experiencing is part of the illness, may further feed your paranoia or create new false beliefs.

The same problem occurs when we try to determine whether a person knows they are hallucinating and seeing, hearing, or feeling things that are not really there. Again, as was evident in my case, this is not as easy to decide as it seems on paper.

What you see, hear, or feel in that state feels so authentic that you become convinced it is real. You may then believe that you are the only one with the ability to perceive things in this new light — that you have been privileged with special insight (e.g., I believed God was showing me a special glimpse of Hell). If this weren't the case, those afflicted wouldn't think or do so many tragic things.

The thoughts experienced in such a state may also be incredibly frightening or shameful (e.g., the thought that my daughter needed to be dead because she was so smart). An afflicted woman often fears that she will be shunned, misunderstood, or permanently locked up if she shares such thoughts with others. Additionally, bizarre thinking patterns will often reside alongside totally logical, rational thinking (e.g., when despite my delusions making me run away, I knew to tell Adam to buckle Lina into her car seat as he chased me). This is often referred to as the "waxing and waning" nature of the illness. This phenomenon will enable a woman with the illness to appear like she is in full possession of her sanity while at the same time exhibiting concerning behaviours and thoughts.

The sad reality of this illness is that the symptoms themselves make it incredibly difficult for the person suffering to identify how sick they really are. Here, the role that family and friends play can save precious lives. It is true that some symptoms, including hallucinations, delusions, and paranoid thoughts, may not be apparent to an outside observer. However, other symptoms, like severe agitation, insomnia, and disorganized speech or bizarre behaviour, may be more obvious and should never be ignored or underestimated.

Although there may be a possibility that PPP subsides on its own after a few months, as happened to me the first time, this can be incredibly dangerous, and leaving the illness alone is never a course of action to follow. It can and has led to the horrific loss of many innocent lives, both mothers and children. In my own experience, it caused me immeasurable suffering that would have been preventable and unknowingly put me at risk after my second pregnancy.

Lastly, it cannot be stressed enough how dangerous it is to leave alone a woman you suspect has PPP. No matter how gentle, kind, or loving a woman is, she is not herself when she has this condition. She cannot be relied upon to make safe decisions for herself or anyone else. There are many women, some of whom I have mentioned in this book, who have committed horrific crimes in the throes of this illness. They should never have been left alone once they were suspected or diagnosed with PPP, even if they had already started receiving treatment. My personal opinion is that doctors should spell out to family *why* a woman with this illness should never be left alone and how dire the consequences can be. Without this knowledge, families might not fully understand why their support and supervision is so necessary.

When unchecked, postpartum psychosis can ravage lives and cause immense pain. When addressed, it is a temporary illness that can be effectively treated. I, and many others, am living proof of that.

ON RACISM IN DIAGNOSING POSTPARTUM MOOD DISORDERS

What happens to women of colour with postpartum mood disorders is not unique and cannot be ignored or downplayed. It is part of a much larger issue: medical racism. This refers to the structural biases and racism that permeate aspects of our lives, including both healthcare practices and systems. This term gives a name to the experiences of Black and other racialized people, who are regularly and callously dismissed as being drug-dependent or are accused of exaggerating their pain when they come in seeking medical aid.

Naming such a phenomenon for what it is, both in the context of postpartum mood disorders and at large in healthcare, is an essential first step toward addressing it.

DISPELLING MYTHS ABOUT POSTPARTUM PSYCHOSIS

Finally, I want to address a few misconceptions family doctors, psychologists, and laypeople may have about PPP.

Myth #1: *If you think you are insane then you are not insane, because psychosis is typified by a lack of insight.*

This is a popular misconception, and one I hope my book has shed light on. An individual may be in total denial that they are ill and psychotic, like I was the first time I had PPP. Alternatively, someone may have a sense they are ill and even "going crazy," but at the same time lack insight into some key symptoms of their illness, including the fact they are hallucinating or delusional, like I was the second time.

If determining insanity was as easy as using the "if you think you are insane" litmus test, psychiatrists wouldn't need the years of training they require.

Myth #2: *It's relatively easy to determine if someone has PPP rather than postpartum obsessive-compulsive disorder based on a simple guideline: if a woman is scared and upset by her thoughts, then she is not suffering from postpartum psychosis.*

I believe anyone who has read my story will easily understand why I find such statements dangerous. It is naive to stick to the notion that if a woman is extremely upset by what she is experiencing, she has not crossed into insanity.

When I went back to look at my medical reports from that time, all I found in them were notations about how insightful and articulate I was and how disturbed and upset I was about my thoughts, as if this was proof of my sanity. Along with ignorance about the condition, this belief also likely played a role in why I didn't get proper treatment, despite going to seek help five times in less than two weeks.

I cannot imagine how many other women there are who may have died or done something they regretted because of this naïveté among healthcare professionals. Anxiety about thoughts does not necessarily prove a woman is sane; the two are not mutually exclusive and can overlap. A woman can be psychotic and yet still be repulsed and made anxious by the thoughts and urges she is experiencing. This was true not only in my case, but with Nadia, who we saw was also upset by her psychotic thoughts and had resolved to kill herself rather than take her child's life.

I would highly recommend that healthcare workers stop trying to simplify a complicated illness. If not for the skilled work of my psychiatrist, I am confident I would not be alive today. Referring a woman to a psychiatrist and erring on the side of caution is always the best course of action.

Myth #3: *Postpartum psychosis is always a variant of bipolar disorder.*

This is true in some, but not all, cases. PPP can also arise out of postpartum depression, as happened to me. The clinical diagnosis for what I experienced both times was "major depressive disorder with psychotic features and postpartum onset," AKA postpartum psychosis. Additionally, even after twenty years, I have never developed any psychiatric symptoms other than those I developed during postpartum.

Viewing PPP as always being a variant of bipolar disorder can result in misdiagnosing women like me, who lacked the mania but suffered from the sadness and ruminations that often characterize severe depression. Treatment is also different based on what the underlying condition is. In my situation, because my PPP stemmed from depression, I didn't need a mood stabilizer. Nadia, however, required a mood stabilizer after hers was later found to be bipolar-based.

I can't help but wonder if the one in ten cases of this illness that end in tragedy might predominantly be cases like mine, which didn't fit the "manic" mold of this illness. Perhaps women whose PPP stems from severe depression have their PPP go unidentified more often and are therefore failed by the system. Perhaps the manic version is easier to notice because it causes more bizarre behaviour. In many of the news stories of infanticide arising from this illness, the women were referred to as severely depressed and zombie-like. Behaviour like that is what my family told me they initially noticed as being wrong with me. Later, they noticed more bizarre behaviour but trusted the doctors who kept advising them that I was doing fine.

Postpartum psychosis is a complicated illness, and oversimplifying it may cause irreversible harm.

Myth #4: *There is nothing worse than being in a mental-health ward.*

I cannot stress enough how much less I would have suffered if I had been admitted into a mental-health ward.

Without a doubt, there are inconveniences to being on such a ward. For example: having your movements restricted, being constantly supervised, and being around people you would rather not be with. However, in my opinion, it is worse to be terrified of yourself or what your life has become, not to mention suffering the isolation of being surrounded by people who don't understand what you are going through and may inadvertently leave you alone.

To me, the option of being admitted temporarily to a mental-health ward is sort of like the epidural conundrum. An epidural, a nerve blocker inserted into your spine to administer pain medication during delivery of a baby, sounds very scary at first. But when you are faced with labour pains, enduring the brief discomfort of an epidural seems like a cake walk. I feel similarly about PPP. The symptoms for which an individual would need to be admitted to such a ward are more frightening than the ward itself.

Myth #5: *Psychiatric medications, especially antipsychotics, are horrible because they make you sluggish, heavy, sleepy, etc.*

No one should judge the side effects of medications without experiencing what they are used to treat. Nobody but the person experiencing the symptoms of an illness and their doctors are in a position to judge the merit of medications, no matter what a drug's side effect profile is.

As was evident from my story, despite the medications causing heaviness and lethargy (terrible-sounding side effects), they were the only things capable of making me feel safe. You may feel you've lost your best friend, sister, or wife to vacant eyes or a lower energy level because of medications. Be grateful you didn't actually lose them to this illness.

Myth #6: *There is nothing worse than suffering from PPP as a new mom.*

There is. And that is suffering and not getting help for its terrifying symptoms. The most important thing to remember is that there *is* help and no one needs to suffer.

Myth #7: *You will never be "normal" again after PPP.*

Postpartum psychosis is a temporary illness, and you can fully recover. It takes time, so you will not be yourself again overnight. But then again, what severe illness can you recover from overnight?

Myth #8: *Women get postpartum mood disorders because motherhood is overwhelming, and some women just aren't cut out for it like the rest of us.*

If anything, I hope my story has dispelled this notion. Honestly, that thought crossed my mind after I went through it the first time. However, I was a secure and confident mother and had a wonderful bond with my daughter by the time PPP hit the second time. There were no nighttime diapers or breastfeeding concerns to contend with, and yet, my second experience of PPP was far worse than the first.

Myth #9: *This is why people should never dabble in drugs or alcohol, because it will make you have illnesses like this.*

I have never touched a cigarette, tried alcohol, or done any recreational drugs. Up until I got sick, the hardest drug to have ever entered my body was Tylenol or Advil. I personally avoid cough syrups containing alcohol and don't even drink an ounce of coffee or tea. Though drugs, including marijuana, may increase the chances of one experiencing a psychotic break, psychosis can happen to anyone.

Myth #10: *Women who experience symptoms like these are possessed.*

If this is what you believe in your heart, there is nothing I can say to change your mind. However, please take a loved one experiencing these symptoms to a reproductive mental-health psychiatrist. They will be able to help with your loved one's suffering. This illness entails much pain, and the least you can do, despite your belief about the nature of this illness, is to alleviate their pain.

HELPFUL RESOURCES ON POSTPARTUM PSYCHOSIS AND POSTPARTUM MOOD DISORDERS

Truth be told, I had many reasons for wanting to write this memoir. Firstly, I wanted to give voice to women who have gone through this frightening experience and not made it out. Another was to humanize those who have committed tragic acts of violence as a result of this illness. I also wanted to show the devastating consequences that ignorance about postpartum psychosis among healthcare providers can have on those struggling.

My ultimate reason, however, was for the wider public to learn about this illness and understand that anyone experiencing its symptoms can be helped. Without a doubt, PPP is one of the most terrifying illnesses in the world today, but it is also a truly treatable one.

. . .

If you suspect someone you know has PPP, take them to your local hospital's emergency department immediately. Do not hesitate.

If you or a loved one would like to speak to a coordinator specializing in PPP, need information, or want support for any type of postpartum mood and anxiety disorder, including PPP, please visit

- postpartum.net

If you want to learn more about PPP and read stories of other women that have recovered from the disorder, please visit

- app-network.org
- mghp3.org

ACKNOWLEDGEMENTS

THESE ARE THE INDIVIDUALS WITHOUT WHOM THIS book would never have been born. They are listed in the order in which they helped bring this to reality.

V.A.K. — For always making me feel I could accomplish anything I set my heart and mind to.

Z.K. — For teaching me to always care for others, which is how this story begins.

Dr. S.E. — I am not sure I would be here today without your astute diagnosis. And when I complained that there were no books out there on this topic, it was you who suggested I write one.

S.A.S. — This book is as much yours as mine for the number of hours you invested into making it a piece worthy of being published. For that, I cannot thank you enough.

A.H.S. — For all the drafts of this you listened to and for being the only one who never doubted that this book would one day be published.

S.K.A. — For being my mentor throughout the process of getting this published. Your wise counsel about ensuring that it offered more than just my story has made this something that will truly shed light on this illness for others.

B.Y. — For being there during the early years of trying to publish this book and supporting me through all my rejections.

M.K., S.K., J.G., A.L. & S.M. — For always praying for me and this project to come to fruition. Well, at least I hope that is what you were doing!

S.H.S. — For being my friend and confidant throughout this publishing process.

J.A.P. — For being my soul sister in PPP advocacy and for being the best cheerleader of my work anyone could ask for.

Dr. Wendy Davis — For being the first person outside of my family to read this book and for making me feel it had value for the wider postpartum community.

Susannah Cahalan — For your advice and support. Not many writers get advice from their favourite author while writing their own book, and I am so grateful to have had yours.

Kathryn Lane — For believing in it, championing it, and seeing this book as worthy of being published.

The Dundurn Team — For helping to make my dream a reality. This team includes Laura Boyle, Erin Pinksen, Megan Beadle, Susan Glickman, and so many more behind the scenes.

NOTES

2: A LITTLE MAD

1   "Key Moments in the Andrea Yates Case," ABC News, January 6, 2005, abcnews.go.com/US/story?id=389198&page=1.

2   "Mom 'Euphoric' Before Baby Died," CBS News, November 23, 2004, cbsnews.com/news/mom-euphoric-before-baby-died.

3   J. Springer, "In Interview, Mother Details Delusions That Spurred Her to Kill Sons," CNN, April 1, 2004, cnn.com/2004/LAW/04/01/laney.

3: I'M POSSESSED

1   Francesca Whiting, "Postpartum Psychosis," Baby Centre, babycentre.co.uk/a1036946/postpartum-psychosis.

2   "Post-partum Psychosis," The Women's, thewomens.org.au/health-information/pregnancy-and-birth/mental-health-pregnancy/post-partum-psychosis.

3   "Postpartum Psychiatric Disorders," MGH Center for Women's Mental Health, womensmentalhealth.org/specialty-clinics/postpartum-psychiatric-disorders.

4   "Data and Statistics on Down Syndrome," Centers for Disease Control and Prevention (CDC), cdc.gov/ncbddd/birthdefects/downsyndrome/data.html.

5   "Prevalence of Cerebral Palsy," CerebralPalsy.org, cerebralpalsy.org
     /about-cerebral-palsy/prevalence-and-incidence.

4: BREATHE

1   Catherine Gigante-Brown, "Postpartum Practices Worldwide: How
     the World Takes Care of Moms and Babies," Ravishly, August 18,
     2015, ravishly.com/2015/08/18/postpartum-practices-worldwide
     -how-world-takes-care-moms-and-babies.
2   Katie Hintz-Zambrano, "Postpartum Care Traditions from Around
     the World," MotherMag, September 28, 2017, mothermag.com
     /postpartum-care-traditions.
3   Sophie Grigoriadis, Gail Erlick Robinson, and Sarah Romans,
     "Traditional Postpartum Practices and Rituals: Clinical
     Implications," *The Canadian Journal of Psychiatry* 54 no.12
     (December 2009): 834–40, doi.org/10.1177/070674370905401206.
4   Anna Abramson and Dawn Rouse, "The Postpartum Brain,"
     Greater Good Magazine, March 1, 2008, greatergood.berkley.edu
     /article/item/postpartum_brain.
5   Alexis Wnuk, "The Postpartum Is a 'Perfect Storm' for
     Depression," BrainFacts.Org, July 6, 2018, brainfacts.org
     /diseases-and-disorders/mental-health/2018/the-postpartum-is-a
     -perfect-storm-for-depression-070618.
6   Abramson and Rouse, "The Postpartum Brain."

9: THE F-WORD

1   "Perinatal Mood and Anxiety Disorders Fact Sheet" (2014),
     Postpartum Support International, postpartum.net/wp-content
     /uploads/2014/11/PSI-PMD-FACT-SHEET-2015.pdf.
2   Tanya Burrwell, "Postpartum Depression and Race: What We
     All Should Know," Psychology Benefits Society, June 21, 2016,
     psychologybenefits.org/2016/06/21/postpartum-depression-in
     -women-of-color.
3   Jamila Taylor and Christy M. Gamble, "Suffering in Silence: Mood
     Disorders Among Pregnant and Postpartum Women of Color,"
     Center for American Progress, November 17, 2017, americanprogress

.org/issues/women/reports/2017/11/17/443051/suffering-in-silence.

4   Kathryn McGrath, "Managing Postpartum Mood Disorders," Lamaze International, lamaze.org/postpartum-blues.

10: ATTENTION GRAB

1   Anna Sandoiu, "Postpartum Depression in Women of Color: 'More Work Needs to Be Done,'" *Medical News Today*, July 17, 2020, medicalnewstoday.com/articles/postpartum-depression -in-women-of-color-more-work-needs-to-be-done.

2   Tanya Burrwell, "Postpartum Depression and Race: What We All Should Know," Psychology Benefits Society, June 21, 2016, psychologybenefits.org/2016/06/21/postpartum-depression-in -women-of-color.

3   Tanya Burrwell, "Postpartum Depression and Race."

12: CINNABON TO THE RESCUE

1   Katy Backes Kozhimannil, Connie Mah Trinacty, Alisa B. Busch, Haiden A. Huskamp, and Alyce S. Adams, "Racial and Ethnic Disparities in Postpartum Depression Care Among Low-Income Women," *Psychiatric Services* 62 no. 6 (2011): 619–25, doi.org /10.1176/appi.ps.62.6.619.

14: KICK THE BASTARD

1   Jamila Taylor and Christy M. Gamble, "Suffering in Silence: Mood Disorders Among Pregnant and Postpartum Women of Color," Center for American Progress, November 17, 2017, americanprogress .org/issues/women/reports/2017/11/17/443051/suffering-in-silence.

15: TAKE TWO ADVILS

1   Suzanne O'Malley, *Are You There Alone?: The Unspeakable Crime of Andrea Yates* (New York: Pocket Star, 2005).
2   "Mom 'Euphoric' Before Baby Died," CBS News, November 23, 2004. cbsnews.com/news/mom-euphoric-before-baby-died.
3   J. Springer, "In Interview, Mother Details Delusions That Spurred Her to Kill Sons," CNN, April 1, 2004, cnn.com/2004/LAW/04 /01/laney.
4   Catherine Cho, *Inferno: A Memoir of Motherhood and Madness* (New York: Henry Holt and Co., 2020).

16: JUMP

1   Jamila Taylor and Christy M. Gamble, "Suffering in Silence: Mood Disorders Among Pregnant and Postpartum Women of Color," Center for American Progress, November 17, 2017, americanprogress .org/issues/women/reports/2017/11/17/443051/suffering-in-silence.
2   "Documents Released in Case of Mother Who Killed and Ate Parts of Son," The Box, July 3, 2010, theboxhouston.com/1269241 /documents-released-in-case-of-mother-who-killed-and-ate-parts -of-son.
3   "Woman Is Committed to State Mental Institution After Killing Her Son," *The Dallas Morning News*, July 2, 2010, dallasnews .com/news/texas/2010/07/02/woman-is-committed-to-state-mental -institution-after-killing-her-son.

20: MY FRIEND MARILYN

1   David Rettew, "Psychiatry's Med Check: Is 15 Minutes Enough?" *Psychology Today*, November 10, 2015, psychologytoday.com /ca/blog/abcs-child-psychiatry/201511/psychiatry-s-med-check -is-15-minutes-enough.
2   Suzanne O'Malley, *Are You There Alone?: The Unspeakable Crime of Andrea Yates* (New York: Pocket Star, 2005).

21: IS THIS YOUR WIFE?

1   Simone Vigod, Anjum Sultana, and Cindy-Lee Dennis, "A Population-Based Study of Postpartum Mental Health Service Use by Immigrant Women in Ontario, Canada," *The Canadian Journal of Psychiatry* 61 no. 11 (2016): 705–13, doi.org/10 .1177/0706743716645285.

2   Tatsuhiko Naito, Justin Chin, Jun Lin, Pritesh J. Shah, and Christine M. Lomiguen, "Postpartum Psychosis in a Non-native Language–Speaking Patient: A Perspective on Language Barriers and Cultural Competency," *General Psychiatry* 32, no. 3 (2019), doi.org/10.1136/gpsych-2019-100077.

22: WAS I LIKE THIS?

1   Jen S. Wight, *Rattled: Overcoming Postpartum Psychosis*, (Tampa, FL: Trigger Publishing, 2019).

2   Patricia Tomasi, "Mom and Baby Units for Postpartum Depression Exist, but Not in Canada," *HuffPost Canada*, October 23, 2018, huffingtonpost.ca/2018/10/22/mom-and-baby-units-canada_a _23566050.

AFTERWORD

1   "Postpartum Psychiatric Disorders," MGH Center for Women's Mental Health, womensmentalhealth.org/specialty-clinics/postpartum -psychiatric-disorders.

2   "Perinatal Mood and Anxiety Disorders Fact Sheet," (2014), Postpartum Support International, postpartum.net /wp-content/uploads/2014/11/PSI-PMD-FACT-SHEET-2015.pdf.

3   "Perinatal Mood and Anxiety Disorders Fact Sheet."

4   Kathryn McGrath, "Managing Postpartum Mood Disorders," Lamaze International, lamaze.org/postpartum-blues.

5   Ian Jones, "Postpartum Psychosis: An Important Clue to the Etiology of Mental Illness," *World Psychiatry* 19 no. 3 (2020): 334–6. ncbi.nlm.nih.gov/pmc/articles/PMC7491647/.

Printed in the USA
CPSIA information can be obtained
at www.ICGtesting.com
JSHW080813091124
73242JS00002B/7

9 781459 754508